UNDERSTANDING
TROPICAL
FISH

INTERPET
HANDBOOKS

UNDERSTANDING
TROPICAL
FISH

GINA SANDFORD

Howell Book House

ISBN: 0-7645-6235-5

Credits

Created and designed: Ideas into Print,
New Ash Green, Kent DA3 8JD, UK.
Computer graphics: Phil Holmes and
Stuart Watkinson
Production management: Consortium,
Poslingford, Suffolk CO10 8RA, UK.
Print production: Sino Publishing
House Ltd., Hong Kong.
Printed and bound in China.

The author

Gina Sandford's interest in fishkeeping
began with a goldfish and developed to
include sticklebacks, young perch, pike
and eventually tropical fish. She has kept
and bred many species, but has a
particular interest in catfishes. She has
written several books and contributed
many articles to magazines and journals.
Gina travels widely, giving audiovisual
presentations and lectures to both
experienced and young audiences.

*Below: Parental care is well developed
among cichlids. Here a mother* Cyrtocara
(Haplochromis) moorii *guards her fry.*

Contents

Introduction

Keeping tropical fish can be a battle or it can be a pleasure. Very often, it is only a battle because we fail to understand the real needs of the fish we are keeping. Although we maintain the temperature, water conditions and lighting levels, sometimes this is just not enough. However, once we start to observe our fish and examine how they are 'built' and how they behave, we begin to acquire a greater insight into their requirements.

First impressions of the shape of the body, the position of the fins, the size of the mouth and the barbels (if present) can be very clear indicators of where in the water column the fish lives, whether it is sedentary or active, what it may or may not eat – even whether it would be a safe addition to a community aquarium or whether it will eat everything else in it!

Although books can describe fish behaviour, it is not until you have kept and observed fish for a while that you begin to find out, say, how territorial they are and how their behaviour affects other fish in the tank. If fish initiate courtship proceedings, note their behaviour and try to provide them with the facilities they need to breed.

When it comes to the internal workings of the fish, most of us would choose to forget them; out of sight, out of mind. However, if we understand how the digestive system of a species works and whether it is a herbivore or an omnivore, we can be sure to provide a suitable diet.

This book will give you an insight into what makes your tropical fish 'tick', so that keeping them becomes an even more rewarding experience.

LIVING IN WATER

Water conditions, chemistry and temperature vary hugely around the world and fish have evolved to occupy every kind of habitat. Appreciating the conditions that prevail in the wild is the first step to successful fishkeeping.

There are thousands of species of fish living in the marine, brackish and fresh waters of the world, in both tropical and temperate conditions. Each requires a given set of parameters to live and reproduce successfully. To keep any of them in the aquarium, it is vital to understand how they function, why they are a certain shape, why they behave as they do, what conditions they need to thrive and how variations can affect them. Armed with this knowledge, you will be able to analyze more confidently the

Diversity of fish habitats

The slow-moving, lower reaches of tropical rivers provide a wide variety of habitats, from dense margins to deep channels for migrating fish.

behaviour and needs of a new or little-known species of fish that you may consider keeping.

What does 'tropical' mean?
The best way to start understanding your tropical fish is to determine what is meant by the term 'tropical'. In the purest sense, it applies to the

portion of the globe that lies between the tropics of Cancer and Capricorn, but things are never that simple. Nature is oblivious to any lines drawn on a map, preferring plants and animals to colonize areas suited to their own requirements for a fruitful life – and temperature may be only one aspect of their needs. Thus, in the tropical freshwater hobby, we have fish available from the tropical and subtropical regions.

The significance of altitude

Latitude is not the only thing that influences water temperature; altitude also plays a part. Fish found in a high mountain stream in, say, Peru, will be living at much lower temperatures than fish at a similar latitude in the mid to lower Amazon Basin. Even within streams, lakes and pools, there can be a diurnal (day-night) fluctuation in water temperature, or thermoclines (layers of water with a steep temperature gradient) that cause no ill-effects to the inhabitants.

Supplying the correct temperature

Being ectothermic (incorrectly described as 'cold-blooded'), fish rely on the warmth of their surroundings to maintain their body temperature and to function at optimum levels. It is the fishkeeper's responsibility to establish their needs

Below: To feel at home in the aquarium, Metynnis lippincottianus *require diffused lighting, plenty of swimming space and water with a gentle current.*

and provide for them. What we really mean by a 'tropical' fish, therefore, is one that requires us to provide some means of ensuring that its captive environment (the aquarium) is maintained at a suitable temperature. In practice, this means using a heater/thermostat to control the water temperature if we live outside the fish's normal range.

Water chemistry

The chemistry of water also varies from place to place. In Africa, the most obvious examples within the hobby are the Rift Lake cichlids that live in hard, alkaline waters, and the small West African dwarf cichlids, which prefer soft, acidic conditions. Although both types belong to the same family, the Cichlidae, it is not possible to keep them in the same

Below: Environments such as this found in Lake Malawi can be easily recreated in the aquarium and will provide a home in which fish are more likely to breed. This is a female Tyranochromis *and her young.*

aquarium and you should never even contemplate the idea. Both incorrect hardness and/or pH levels can have an adverse effect on a fish's metabolism. Although both can be adjusted to a degree (and any such adjustments should always be made gradually), in some cases it may be impossible to acclimatize a particular species to aquarium conditions.

Fish found in fast-flowing streams or rapids require high oxygen levels to survive. Usually, these waters are also cool. Fish from swampy regions are at the other end of the range; their water is much warmer and has a lower oxygen content.

How fish adapt to water conditions

Water is much denser than air; you have only to wade through it to feel the extra effort required to walk just a short distance. Fish have come to terms with this, and their body shape, fin shapes and positions, and mouth types can be a valuable clue to their natural home. Hillstreams may be slow flowing in the dry seasons,

Above and right: Swift hill streams have highly oxygenated waters that may be cooler than expected. In the home aquarium, you will need temperature control and an external power filter to provide enough water movement for fish such as this streamlined Pseudogastromyzon.

but during the rains they become raging torrents that carry silt and rocks down to the main rivers. Fishes living in these conditions often have flattened bodies, and mouths or finnage that have been developed into some form of sucker to help anchor them firmly to a rock or log and prevent them being washed away in the torrent. Some catfish, loaches and balitorids are typical of fish found in such areas.

By contrast, the slow-moving waters of the lower reaches and backwaters of rivers are home to fish with laterally compressed bodies, such as discus, that would be swept away with the swirling water in fast-flowing streams.

Even seasonal pools can harbour fish, and the annual killifishes have exploited this niche. Males have developed extended, flamboyant finnage and the fish have become very popular in the hobby. In the wild, there are no water currents to sweep them away and if they are kept in an aquarium with too great

Above: To keep and breed annual
killifish, such as this Nothobranchius
rachovi, *successfully you must meet their
very specific requirements. But a little
research will pay ample dividends.*

a water flow, the fish will become
unsettled and stressed.

Caves and sink holes also provide
homes for fish. The best known of
these in the hobby is *Astyanax
fasciatus mexicanus*, the blind cave
fish, but there are more than 40
other species of cave fish, all of
which have evolved to cope with this
demanding lifestyle (see page 79).

Reflecting the natural environment
Within any body of water there will
be different environments. Some are
defined by the substrate, which could
be rocky, sandy or weedy; some by
water flow, such as an open river
channel or small, almost still,
backwater; and some by depth –
lakes, for example – or a
combination of all these. Fish will
colonize the areas most suited to

their needs, and to keep them
successfully we must try to replicate
the ideal conditions. However,
providing a species with a 4m (13ft)-
deep tank is beyond most fishkeepers
and what we think of as shallows are
not necessarily what the fish consider
them to be. How fortunate for us
that many fish are adaptable when it
comes to the depth of water that they
can live and reproduce in.

Researching the needs of a
particular species is important for its
well-being. Take the loach that likes
to bury in the substrate, searching for

Life at the edge

Think of an aquatic habitat and
there will be a fish that lives in it.
At the extremes, fish are found in
the Arctic Circle, where the waters
freeze in the winter, and also in hot
springs, where temperatures can
reach over 38°C (100°F).

food and hiding from predators. If you place that fish in a bare tank or one with large pebbles for a substrate, it becomes stressed because it cannot function normally. The same can be said for any fish whose needs are not catered for. These fish then become susceptible to infections, just the response that aquarists, wish to avoid. With a little thought, we can create a tangle of roots, leaf litter, cave structures, rocky shores, plant thickets, open substrate areas, even open water for swimming, which can make all the difference to the fishes

in our care. And combinations of substrates and habitat areas enable us to keep fishes with differing lifestyles in the same aquarium.

By simple analysis, it is possible to determine and then meet the needs of most aquarium fish. The reward is a healthy aquarium full of contented fish that are more likely to breed.

Below: Even something as simple as keeping shoaling fish in large enough groups can make the difference between success and failure. With companions, these Botia sidthimunki *will thrive.*

FIRST IMPRESSIONS

It is hard to imagine the effort required to move in water, a medium that is 800 times denser than air. All aquatic organisms encounter this problem, and they have adapted to operate efficiently and with the minimum of effort.

Streamlined for stability

Most sedentary, bottom-dwelling fish, such as this royal farlowella, have a hydrodynamically shaped, triangular body cross-section.

Most constantly swimming fish have a uniform, more-or-less torpedo-shaped body that is described as fusiform. It reduces to a minimum the effect of drag on the fish – the consequence of water passing over the body, fins and any other external feature. The drag will always be there, but can be greatly reduced by variations in body form and finnage.

Variations in body shape
Of course, there are huge variations in body shape. Not all fish have a fusiform body shape, but there again,

many fish do not swim constantly or live in strong water currents. They may lead a more sedentary lifestyle. Take, for example, the angelfish and discus. Their body is flattened laterally, and described as compressed. Viewed from the side, it is roughly circular. This is not a body shape best suited to strong currents,

Right: The hatchetfish (Gasteropelecus sternicla), *is a surface dweller that often makes aerial leaps to catch low-flying insects. To help the fish achieve this, the 'breast', or sternum, is large and keel-like, with powerful pectoral muscles attached to it.*

where the large body surface area greatly increases drag. Indeed these fish tend to inhabit mid-layers of still waters, where their compressed bodies allow them to manoeuvre easily amongst sturdy plant stems, despite their relatively large size.

Other fish have a flattened body form, otherwise referred to as depressed, where the body is wide, but shallow in depth. These fish are generally bottom-dwellers. They include some catfish, such as *Chaca*, the frogmouth catfish. For them, agility is not vital, but concealment is paramount.

Many other bottom-dwellers have a body form that is roughly triangular in cross-section, or at least considerably flattened on the underside. This gives them some stability as they lie on the substrate. It also means that the body is pushed down onto the substrate as the water current passes over it. This stabilizing force is generally enhanced by paired fins, often broad, fanlike structures, horizontally placed, and in many instances supported by a thickened leading ray. Loaches and many catfish are prime examples of this body form.

In many surface-dwelling fish, the body is flattened along the dorsal (top) surface. The mouth is invariably placed dorsally. These fish can easily feed from foods at, or even slightly above, the water surface (see page 80/How fish feed). There are a great number of examples; many killifish, the hatchetfish (*Gasteropelecus*) that leaps from the water to capture low-flying insects, the archerfish (*Toxotes*), with its splendidly accurate spitting aim that dislodges bugs and insects from overhanging tree branches, and the powerful arowana, which can leap 1m (39in) or more into the air to capture much larger prey. The main concern of surface-dwelling fish is to ensure concealment from terrestrial predators. Long, flowing or high dorsal fins would stick above the water surface and advertise their presence, so these are greatly reduced in height.

Elongate, eel-like body shapes are ideally suited to fish that live among plant and submerged tree roots on the substrate. In these fish, the finnage is somewhat reduced in size, with little of the flamboyance seen in

Below: The African reedfish (Erpetoichthys calabaricus) *has an elongate, sinuous body covered with trapezoidal ganoid scales. It is mainly active at night and slides like a snake amongst vegetation on the riverbed.*

other fish. Tropical examples include the African reedfish *(Erpetoichthys calabaricus)* and some gobies (such as *Gobioides broussoneti).*

Body coverings

As well as skin, many, but by no means all, fish are covered in scales or bony plates. As we shall see, there is a distinct difference between these coverings. In fish that are just covered in skin, this is usually thick and tough.

Scales

The most common form of covering is scales. These may cover the entire body and head or be limited in extent. The number of scales on a fish can vary greatly in both size and quantity. (The number and arrangement of the scales is referred to as squamation, and can be used as a basis for identification.) There are

Above: The hard, enamelled ganoid scales on this spotted gar (Lepisosteus oculatus) *reveal its ancient origins. They form a flexible suit of armour.*

Right: Most freshwater tropical fish have cycloid scales. As their name suggests, they are circular, although only part of each is visible as they overlap. Cycloid scales have rings that reflect seasonal patterns of growth.

three main types of scale, each found on different fish. Ganoid scales are roughly trapezoidal in shape, with a small extension in one corner. The outer layer of these scales is covered in a thick layer of ganoine, a hard enamel-like material. This type of scale is particularly thick and found on more ancient fish, such as bichirs and African reedfish.

Cycloid scales are the most commonly encountered and so-called due to their roughly circular form. This type of scale is found on characins, cyprinids and many cichlids and is the one that best shows the seasonal growth cycles.

The third type of scale is ctenoid (the 'c' is silent). These scales have a comblike fringe at the trailing edge. Examples include the aptly named *Ctenopoma* (African bushfish).

Cycloid and ctenoid scales are fairly flexible, and because they overlap, only about 25% of the scale is visible externally, in much the same way as tiles on a roof. As the fish grows, so do the scales. In good seasons, when food is plentiful, the fish and the scales grow at a greater rate. This seasonal growth can be seen as growth rings on the scales, although some magnification will be needed to see this on small fish.

Left: These are ctenoid scales, with the typical comblike fringe clearly visible on the trailing edges. They are best seen on the African bushfish (Ctenopoma sp.).

Below: This corydoras catfish, Corydoras rabauti, has bony plates instead of scales. They partially or entirely cover some catfishes and are formed in the early stages of development by the skin wrinkling and ossifying into bone.

Bony plates

Bony plates, as found on some catfish such as *Corydoras*, are very different from scales. When the fish first hatch they lack any plates, but in the early stages of development, the skin folds along the body and gradually hardens into bony plates. These plates can be quite thick, so much so that the lateral line pits (see page 76) cannot penetrate the plates. Instead, the lateral line pits are located just where successive plates overlap, so that their function is not impeded.

The purpose of scales and plates

Moving in water, which is hundreds of times denser than air, is extremely difficult. Overlapping scales help the underlying muscle segments to produce the sinuations of the body that give the fish a swimming action (see page 33 for more details). There is also a strong possibility that scales help to reduce drag.

Scales, in particular, are somewhat fragile, and while in most species they can regenerate, they do not necessarily protect the fish in certain adverse conditions. Take, for example, bottom-dwelling fish that are subjected to buffeting currents that can dash them against debris or the substrate. Often, in these fish the area of the body normally covered by scales is either greatly reduced or there are no scales at all, and the naked skin is greatly thickened to afford protection. This is seen in many catfish, including bagrids and pimelodids. The naked skin is often more thickly covered in mucus to give added protection against disease caused by damage. The mucus also acts as a lubricant between the fish and the surrounding water. In the cyprinid *Gyrinocheilus*, the so-called Chinese algae-eater that lives in fast-flowing hillstreams, the upper part of the body is covered in scales, but there are none on the underside, the part of the body most vulnerable to damage from the environment.

Of course, those fish with an ample covering of bony plates are even better protected, not just from harsh environments, but also to a limited extent, from predation. However, all this extra protection comes at a cost. The ability to flex the body – essential in long, continuous swimming – is reduced, and the additional weight of the bony plates also slows down the fish.

Coloration

Within the skin are pigmentation cells that give fish a variety of colours. Without these cells the fish would be flesh-coloured, just like unpigmented cave fish (see page 79). There are two main types of cell that produce colour. The chromatophores contain pigments of different hues. When varying pigments in adjacent cells mix, like an artist mixing paints, more colour variations are created. The intensity of colour can also be controlled by concentrating or diluting the pigments.

The other form of pigment cells are iridocytes which, as the name suggests, impart a degree of iridescence, or sparkle, to the colour. The prime constituent is waste material of the blood system.

Many fry have little pigmentation; their bodies are often virtually transparent – an ideal form of concealment in the first few days of life. Some other fry are similar in colour to their surroundings, only developing the vibrancy of the adults as they grow and are better able to defend themselves.

Body shape and colour in action

Fish use colour in a variety of ways. Many fish, particularly midwater and upper-layer swimmers, have a basic countershaded form to the body, whereby the dorsal surface is a dull grey-brown and the underside is silvery-white. This is common to most fish, even in those that appear quite colourful from the side. If you look at your fish from above, you will notice two things. The fish is not

Above: The coloration of this angelfish looks most striking in the aquarium, but in the dappled light of its natural environment the vertical bars help to conceal the fish as its swims slowly among tall plant stems and twigs.

only much harder to spot, but also more difficult to identify, because all the other fish have a similar dorsal colour. This also makes it harder for predators above the water surface to find their prey, as the dull coloration helps the fish to merge with the substrate. Bear in mind that natural predation of freshwater fish is primarily from terrestrial and particularly aerial vertebrates. Conversely, the silvery-white underside, when viewed from below, merges well with the brightly lit water surface.

It is not surprising, therefore, that most bottom-dwelling fish are fairly dark in colour, particularly as in many cases the body is moderately compressed. Seen from above, the dark colour merges well with the surroundings and is the reason why many catfish (which are principally bottom-dwellers anyway) lack the resplendent hues of other fish.

Confusing spots and stripes

Most vivid coloration is limited to the lateral surfaces of a fish and has a wide range of different functions.

Shoaling fish often display a recognisable colour pattern or spot at the base of the caudal fin, or more commonly, stripes or a large elongate mark on one or both lobes of the caudal fin. These help the fish to identify rapid changes in direction of the shoal, acting like tail lights of a car at night as it travels the congested highways.

Single, large, colourful iridescent spots with a dark border (called ocelli), again placed near the hind end of the fish, are used to confuse a predator into believing that it is seeing the eye of its prey. The luckless predator is then most perplexed when the prey swims in the opposite direction to that of the false eye end, and the potential prey lives to see another day.

Some egglaying African cichlids use spots to induce fertilisation in the spawning ritual. The spots, usually between two and five and the same size and colour as the eggs to be laid, are placed on the anal fin, immediately behind the vent (see page 106).

Colour and pattern are also used to 'break up' the shape of the fish through what can only be described as visual confusion. This occurs a great deal in marine reef fish, but is

Above: Spots on the anal fin of this male *Aulonocara* hueseri *look like eggs. Instead of picking up these false eggs, the female collects milt (sperm) with which to fertilize the eggs carried in her mouth.*

also seen in some freshwater species. The intention is to create false bands of shadow using dark bands that do not follow the general shape or outline of the fish.

Vertical dark bars are oftenfound on fish that spend much of their time amongst dense vegetation, while the lighter parts between the bars merge with the stems of the plants. Angelfish *(Pterophyllum)*, discus *(Symphysodon)* and some barbs are examples of this form of coloration.

Netlike, reticulated patterning is often seen on fish that live in shallow, fast-flowing waters, where dappled sunlight penetrates the surface. Examples here are some of the hillstream danios and the royal plec *(Panaque nigrolineatus)*.

Warning colours

Coloration can also be used as an advertisement, as a warning or to attract a mate. Venomous fish are often garishly coloured, as are some spiny fish. A predator will only attempt to capture these fish once; after that initial experience, it will quickly recognise them by their colour and avoid them in future confrontations.

Sexual coloration

In many fish, coloration intensifies at the outset of spawning to attract a member of the opposite sex. This is generally (but not always) more likely to happen in males, the winners being the ones with the most flamboyant display. The variation between the normal coloration and the mating spectacle can be quite

Above: Dappled patterning is often seen in fish living in shallow, fast-flowing water. The effect matches the dappling created as sunlight filters down through the moving water in which they swim.

marked, but it is vital for attracting the healthiest mate. However, it can be a risky business as it may also attract the unwanted attentions of passing predators. Often, the fins are also called into action to enhance the display and are intensely coloured during this activity.

Day and night colour changes

One little-known fact is that many freshwater fish change colour and/or pattern during the night. A prime example of this is the pencilfish

Left: This is a male cherry barb (Barbus titteya) *showing the intense red colour that it adopts as spawning time approaches.*

Right: Although by no means plain, the female cherry barb does not show the intensity of colour seen in the breeding male. Such sexual coloration is common in the world of tropical fish.

(*Nannostomus* and *Nannobrycon* spp.). The reasons are not fully established, but it could be an energy efficiency measure. (This is comparable to a screen saver on a computer monitor.) After all, energy derived from food is required in the generation of colour. Virtually all cave-dwelling fish that live in perpetual darkness have lost all pigmentation, probably for the same reasons. Some cave fish (and there are over 40 true cave-dwelling species) are fairly 'new' (in evolutionary terms) to this existence or live near the mouth of the cave. These fish often display only weak pigmentation. If they are then placed into an artificially lit environment, some regeneration of the pigment cells may occur.

Masters of disguise

Often, colour and body shape combine effectively to help a fish disguise itself. A good freshwater example of this is the South American leaf-fish, *Monocirrhus polycanthus*. Its body is greatly

Above: This daytime colour pattern on these pencilfishes (Nannobrycon eques) changes at night to a darker background with two broad transverse bars.

compressed (flattened laterally) and shaped like a leaf, even down to the leaf stem – a short appendage on the lower jaw. In addition, its colour resembles that of a mottled brown dead leaf. Drifting in the water currents, it goes unnoticed by the hapless fish on which it preys.

A similar situation exists in many of the banjo catfish, found principally in the tropical forest creeks of northern South America, although here it works to protect the fish from predation. They, too, look like dead leaves and live among true fallen leaves. Even when they are picked up and released in an aquarium, they simply drift back onto the substrate, rather than make a mad dash for cover. Another example is *Farlowella*, the twig catfish, which is both shaped and coloured like a piece of dead twig in the water. It goes largely unmolested

Above: *The leaflike body shape and colour, together with its habit of 'drifting' along in a gentle current, helps the leaf fish* (Monocirrhus polycanthus) *remain undetected as it seeks out its prey.*

Below: *The twig catfish* (Farlowella *sp.*) *certainly resembles a twig, but this time the camouflage is not for hunting but for concealment from predators in the waters of their South American river homes.*

as it feeds on algae. In fact, many sedentary catfish have evolved bizarre body forms that do an enormously good job of concealment.

Fish that live near the surface, such as hatchetfish (*Gasteropelecus*), are often silvery coloured, so as not to draw attention to themselves. They are also fairly flat along the back, so that only the dorsal fin penetrates the water surface. The mouth is also adjacent to the surface, so that it can easily engulf any insect that falls onto the water. Other surface-dwellers, such as the freshwater butterflyfish (*Pantodon*), sport a brown-marbled pattern, emulating tree debris floating on the water.

Brightly coloured fish

Of course, there are exceptions to the widespread use of colour and pattern as concealment or camouflage. Even though they are mainly surface-dwellers, many of the killifish have intense hues. However, they often live in small, temporary bodies of water, with a greatly reduced, if not absent, population of predatory fish. (But birds, the prime vertebrate predators of fish, are ever-present.) Because of the temporary seasonal existence of the water, which often limits killifish lifespan to much less than a year, the fish must quickly breed and lay their eggs. It is the brilliant hues used by the males that attract a suitable female with which to breed.

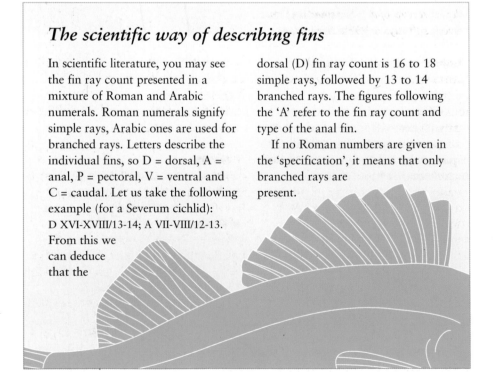

The scientific way of describing fins

In scientific literature, you may see the fin ray count presented in a mixture of Roman and Arabic numerals. Roman numerals signify simple rays, Arabic ones are used for branched rays. Letters describe the individual fins, so D = dorsal, A = anal, P = pectoral, V = ventral and C = caudal. Let us take the following example (for a Severum cichlid): D XVI-XVIII/13-14; A VII-VIII/12-13. From this we can deduce that the dorsal (D) fin ray count is 16 to 18 simple rays, followed by 13 to 14 branched rays. The figures following the 'A' refer to the fin ray count and type of the anal fin.

If no Roman numbers are given in the 'specification', it means that only branched rays are present.

Above: The ancient bichirs (Polypterus sp.) have what appears to be a very spiny dorsal fin that almost joins the caudal fin.

Right: On closer inpection, the dorsal fin is seen to be composed of a series of finlets made up of a single spine with one or more soft rays on the trailing edge.

Colour and pattern for mimicry

Amongst some fish, mimicry is an excellent form of protection. The South American *Corydoras* catfish is partly protected by bony plates, but also sports strong, sharp, leading fin spines to the dorsal and pectoral fins, which makes it more than a mouthful for any predator. There are numerous *Corydoras* species – well over 120 – but one species is mimicked by a characin that lacks the bony plates and fin spines, but is identical in colour and size. This is not just a random likeness, because the characin shoals amongst the *Corydoras* and benefits from this protective mimicry.

A similar situation exists in Asia, where a cyprinid mimics a small but spiny catfish. Aquarium observations confirm the mutual trust between these disparate fish, although how the catfish benefits from the mimicry, if at all, is unclear.

The fins

Perhaps the most obvious features of any fish are its fins. Sometimes they are short, sometimes long, in some cases irregularly shaped, often diaphanous, and varied in position, number and form. All fish have fins of one sort or another. They not only play a functional role in the movement of a fish, but may also be used as an attractive display in courtship and breeding. Conversely, they may be used as a warning display to others. Some fins are used

The full set of fins

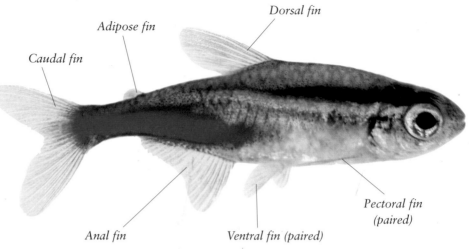

Caudal fin

Adipose fin

Dorsal fin

Anal fin

Ventral fin (paired)

Pectoral fin (paired)

for defence or even as a means of injecting venomous substances into would-be predators. Fins can also be used to fan well-oxygenated water over tended eggs, or as a means of transferring sticky eggs from the vent to a suitable surface.

The anatomy of the fins

Mostly, fins are made up of a thin flap of skin supported by bony rays. When they are first born, most fish have a continuous flap of skin that runs from just behind the head, around the tail and along the underside. As the fish develops, this flap of skin separates to form the median fins, and in the process, fin rays develop to support them.

Inside the fish, at the fin base, the rays are attached to muscles that allow the fin to move mainly longitudinally, but also to a very limited degree, from side to side. Any damage to the fine membrane of skin

will normally heal and regenerate, provided that the damage was not caused by disease. Fin rays can also regrow should the need arise. The membrane may be transparent or coloured.

The supporting fin rays may be simple (unbranched), branched or fused to form a spine. There may be a mixture of fin rays in a fin; the number of simple rays, or spines, and branched rays can help in the identification of many species. For example, in cichlids (and other members of the Perciformes group) the first portion of the dorsal fin is supported by simple hard rays, and the hind part by softer, branched rays (see page 30).

Median fins

Fins can be grouped into two forms: median and paired. Median fins are found along the middle of the fish. These are the dorsal fin or fins along the back, the anal fin on the underside (so-called because it is just behind the fish's vent), and the caudal, or tail, fin. Depending on species, there may also be an adipose fin just behind the dorsal fin (see page 35). Median fins are also known as unpaired, or vertical, fins.

Paired fins

The paired fins occur on both sides of the body. These are the pectoral fins (equivalent to arms) near the gill covers (operculum) at the back of the head, and the ventral fins a little further along the side, often just in front of the vent. The ventral fins are often orientated

vertically, but in many bottom-dwelling fish are placed horizontally. Ventral fins are sometimes described as pelvic fins. Both terms are correct, but in this book we will refer to them as ventral fins. Like the pectoral fins, these are usually, but not always, held vertically.

The function of the fins

Each fin has a role to play in the movement of a fish, and also helps it retain its position against the water currents. However, in most cases, the fins are not used for constant swimming. This is achieved by wavelike movements of the body. The prime motive force of a fish – its equivalent to first

Fins in action

The paired pectoral fins help with fine positional movements.

A flick of the caudal fin gets the fish moving and sinuations of the body keep it going.

The dorsal fin is clearly flexing as the fish turns and, together with the anal fin, acts as a keel.

The paired pelvic fins stabilize the fish and help to prevent the head dipping in a pitching motion.

The anal fin works like a keel to reduce rolling.

Above: Not only does this hillstream Gastromyzon *have a streamlined body form, but the pectoral and ventral fins also form a large suction pad on its underside to help it maintain its position.*

gear in a car – is the caudal, or tail, fin. Its shape can influence its effectiveness, as we shall see later on. Once the caudal fin has created the initial impetus to get the fish moving, further forward movement is achieved by the body flexing from side to side as momentum increases. The caudal fin can also be used as a rudder to help steer the fish when it is travelling at speed.

The dorsal and anal fins (the other two median fins) act as a keel, similar to that found on boats, and prevent the fish rolling and moving from side to side (yawing). This requires constant fine adjustments to the median fin surfaces.

The paired fins have a multitude of uses. In order to brake or decelerate, the pectoral fins are extended out from the body. At this time, the ventral fins' role is to prevent pitching, the action that causes the body to pitch nose up or

down. The paired fins, particularly the pectorals, are also used for fine manoeuvring at low speed, and help to keep the fish stationary in moving water currents.

Moving to stay still

Some fish, notably some cyprinids such as barbus and rasbora, as well as small characins, seem to twitch constantly when at rest in the midwater level of the aquarium. This is due to the fact that for every action there is an equal and opposite reaction. In this case, the action is the expulsion of water from the gill chamber, which causes the fish to move forward. To compensate, the fish uses its pectoral fins to 'backpedal', in synchronization with its respiration. This is just one more function of the pectoral fins.

The adipose fin

Strictly speaking, the adipose is not a fin in the sense that it provides motive, or directional, control, although in some species it may act as a rudimentary keel. Instead, it is primarily a store of fatty tissue.

Observing fin movement

To increase your understanding of the functions of the fins, observe some of the slow-moving fish, such as anabantids and many cichlids,

Below: The freshwater butterflyfish (Pantodon) *uses its winglike pectoral fins to generate momentum to help it leap up and catch insects above the water surface.*

which seem to move with a certain deliberation. You will begin to appreciate the form and function of each fin, how it relates to the other fins and the movements of the fish.

Fins as hydrodynamic features

Given the tens of thousands of different freshwater fish around the world, it is not surprising that some have developed similar fin forms and functions in relation to their lifestyle. As we have seen, the paired fins – the pectorals and ventrals – of many bottom-dwelling fish are held horizontally rather than vertically, as is generally the case with fish from higher levels of the water column. Often, these bottom-dwellers lead a sedentary lifestyle, where constant swimming is not a regular activity. However, water flowing over the

beds of streams and rivers can create strong swirling currents as it passes around rocks and other obstacles. The need to prevent being swept away is of paramount importance to these fish. Horizontally orientated paired fins can be angled to produce a hydrodynamic surface that uses the current to push the fish down, in much the same way as aerodynamic 'wings' fitted to high-speed racing cars help to keep the wheels in contact with the road. Often, in these circumstances, the leading fin ray is thickened, making it possible for the fish to anchor itself among the rocks.

In other bottom-dwelling fish, such as *Gastromyzon*, the pectoral and ventral fins are not only placed horizontally, they are also joined together to form a large suction cup. This is yet another way in which the fish are prevented from being washed away in the strong hillstream currents in which they live.

'Flying' fish

Some surface-dwelling fish also have large, fanlike pectoral fins that are horizontally placed and positioned towards the upper sides of the fish. The freshwater butterflyfish (*Pantodon*) is one example. When beaten vigorously, the pectoral fins help the fish leap above the water to catch the low-flying insects on which it thrives. The fins are not used for aerial flight, but to gain momentum before leaving the water. To power the fins, the pectoral girdle is formed into a deep ridge that provides an anchorage for the powerful muscles required to operate them.

Other unusual fin forms

The ancient Australian lungfish (*Neoceratodus forsteri*) has a peculiar structure to its pectoral fins, whereby the fin rays radiate from a central bony core. The surrounding tissue is thick and fleshy. The ventral fin is somewhat similar, and could be interpreted as an early development of the limbs of prototype terrestrial creatures.

In some instances, two or all three of the median fins are fused into a long single fin. The gymnarchid eels have fused dorsal and caudal fins, and in some species, the anal fin is also fused. These fish send a wave or series of waves along the length of these long-based fins to achieve controlled slow-speed motion, both forwards and backwards.

The ancient group of freshwater bichirs are also worthy of note. In these fish, the dorsal consists not of a continuous fin, but of a number of smaller finlets, between five and fifteen, depending on species. Each has a leading spine, with support rays extending from it rather than from the body of the fish

Fin size and shape

The area of the fin surfaces has a great effect on the ability of the fish to move through the water. A large fin area in relation to body size can create considerable drag. This is not a feature that will be of concern to slow-moving fish or those that only swim for short periods, but it can severely impede shoaling fish.

Slower-moving or sedentary fish generally have a large caudal fin,

Body shape, turbulence and drag

1 2 3

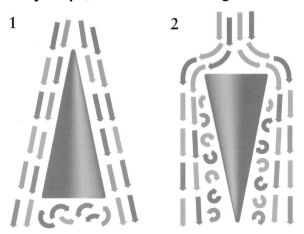

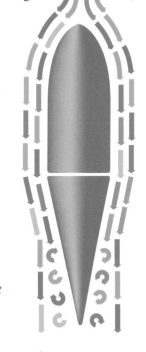

Streamlining is clearly important for fish. These simple shapes illustrate the relationship of turbulence and drag. Surprisingly, the eddies behind a cone with its apex facing into the water flow (1) create more drag than if the cone is positioned with its base facing into the flow (2). Combining the two shapes into something resembling a fish (3) reduces both the turbulence and drag to much lower levels.

Caudal fins for speed and duration

The deeply forked caudal fin is ideal for sustained stretches of swimming and is widely seen on shoaling fishes.

A rounded caudal fin is typical of fish that put on a sudden burst of speed to seek out food or avoid predation.

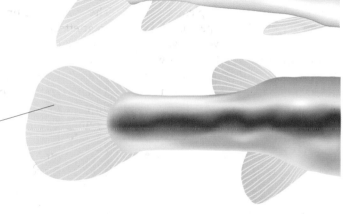

37

often truncate, rounded or only slightly notched around the margin. This is totally unsuited for sustained swimming due to the high drag factor. The base of the caudal is thickened by the underlying muscles. Caudal fins of this type are ideally suited to the short, sharp bursts of swimming energy needed for a rapid retreat from predators or other dangers, or simply to make a quick lunge at dinner!

Deeply forked, or lunate, caudal fins are more closely associated with species that constantly swim or shoal. As these fins are quite short, although possibly also deep, drag resistance is much reduced. Rapid starts from a stationary position are not so easy to achieve, but then these fish are generally always moving in relation to the surrounding water currents. Fish with these types of caudal fin shapes can often appear to be motionless, but are in effect maintaining station in the current, positioning themselves with their heads into the water current. When viewed from above, they can be seen flexing their bodies in a constant sinuous swimming action.

Fin spines, locking mechanisms and other fin adaptations

Some fish are endowed with powerful fin spines at the leading edge of the dorsal and/or pectoral fins. These are more than just a simple fin ray; they are immensely strong, often sharp at the far end, and sometimes armed with sawtooth edges. The prime exponent of these stout fin spines are the catfish.

Over great periods of time, catfish have developed functions that best suit their environment. Although they are for the most part bottom-dwellers, fin functions that are better

Right: Once locked upright, the dorsal spine of this Amblydoras hancocki *cannot be lowered unless the fish wishes. This makes the fish a difficult mouthful and forms an excellent wedge in crevices.*

deployed by pelagic, or midwater, swimmers have evolved to a remarkable degree. Virtually all fish have a leading spine to the dorsal and pectoral fins, but in the case of the catfish, these spines are also equipped with a mechanically positive locking mechanism. When in use, it allows the spines to be deployed erect. In this state, the spines cannot be lowered by any external intervention, only by the voluntary action of the fish itself.

The locking dorsal fin

The mechanisms employed in locking the spines are unique and so finely engineered that they deserve further examination. The dorsal fin spine of a catfish has a bony locking pin at its base. This is easy to see on many of the larger catfish; from the outside, it

looks like a triangular plate, but internally it is forked, with prongs that fit into a saddle at the rear of the skull. Ligaments connect the skull to the locking pin, and further ligaments link the pin with the fin spine. As the spine is erected, the same ligaments draw the pin down into the saddle grooves. Once in place, the locking pin prevents the dorsal fin spine from lowering.

Often, the catfish will die with the dorsal spine erect and locked, almost as though this is an involuntary action on death. With care, you can pull the dorsal spine slightly up and away from the body. It will in turn lift the locking pin out of engagement, allowing you to lower the spine. You cannot now relock the mechanism, as all control of the necessary muscles is lost.

The locking pectoral fin

The pectoral fin locking mechanism is even more refined. There is no locking pin; instead, the fin spine articulates in a finely engineered ball and socket joint (like a hip joint). The ball is at the base of the spine and the socket is on the pectoral girdle, which can generally be seen through the thin overlaying skin, traversing the underside of the head and linking the two pectoral fin bases. The pectoral fin spine is capable of moving both forwards and backwards, as well as tilting the front edge approximately 30-45° downwards about the spine axis.

With the spine horizontal, the ball freely articulates forwards and back, but as the spine tilts on its axis the ball seizes in the socket, effectively locking it in any desired position. (In this respect it differs from the dorsal spine, which can only be locked in the fully erect position.)

Again, investigating a dead catfish can be quite instructive – and not just to demonstrate how sharp the fin spines can be! By twisting the pectoral spine, it is possible to lock and release the lock, and unlike the dorsal spine, this can be repeated time and again. But do take care; the fin spines are extremely sharp.

How fish use their fin spines

Lockable fin spines have many advantages. They allow a catfish to burrow into a hollow and expand its spines against the walls of its retreat. With the fin spines then locked, it is well and truly secured. Similarly, the fish can gain purchase among stones and boulders to prevent it being swept away by the current.

Erecting and locking the spines can effectively increase the size of the catfish, with the added advantage that the spine tips are distinctly sharp, presenting a considerable challenge to any predator looking for an easy meal. And fish are not the only predators; probably by far the greatest toll on fish in their natural environment comes from birds. They, too, can find eating spiny catfish somewhat difficult. Kingfishers, for example, remove the spines first by flailing the hapless catfish against a rock or tree, before swallowing and digesting their meal.

The African clarias catfish uses its fin spines in the course of overland migration to other, unconnected bodies of water. This migration becomes necessary when the water in which it is living dries out, which happens periodically, and the fish needs to find fresh water to survive. The fin spines are used to pull the clarias catfish along as it makes sinuous movements with its body. These migrations usually take place at night, when the climate is not harsh enough to dry out the fish and there is far less risk of predation.

Some catfish also use the pectoral spines in a scissor action against the sides of the body. The doradids, the group of so-called talking cats, often have serrated leading and trailing edges to the pectoral spine which mesh nicely with the row of thorny plates down each side of the body. Are they effective? Well, just ask any catfish enthusiast to relate his or her experiences when handling these fish – or look for the telltale scars!

The effect of these serrations on a would-be enemy can be profound.

Below: Many tropical and coldwater fish are armed with sharp spines and serrations that can easily cut the fingers of unwary aquarists! These are the dorsal scutes of a sturgeon.

The sharp point at the end of the spine can enter the aggressor, and the subsequent damage can aggravate the wound significantly.

Handle with care
Sometimes, fin spines can do more than just puncture an aggressor (and this does not apply solely to the spines of catfish). Fish are liberally covered with mucus, and this includes the fin spine. Should this mucus enter the bloodstream of an attacker, a reaction may occur in the form of blood poisoning, which can be quite painful and may lead to temporary numbness. Fish with the capacity to inflict this sort of injury must be handled with respect, as they can poison people, too, with quite acute results.

In some cases, spines have a true venom reservoir in a sac underlying the thin skin covering. Once the skin and the sac are ruptured, the venom is free to flow into the open wound. The physical effects of this can be far more unpleasant than those described above. They can vary according to species, as the chemical compounds of the venom differ.

UNDER THE SKIN

Below the skin of a fish, the first thing you see are its muscles. These are attached to the skeleton, and tucked away inside the body cavity are the swimbladder and all the other internal organs that keep the fish functioning.

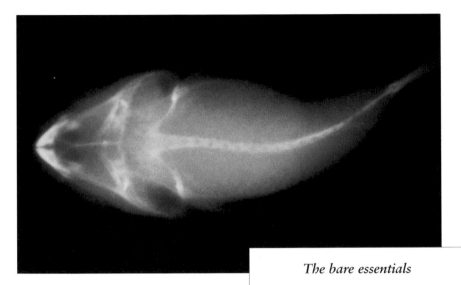

The bare essentials

An X-ray clearly reveals the jaw bones, gill arches and flexible backbone of this tropical fish. These form the basic supporting framework.

The fish's skeleton forms a firm foundation that supports and protects the soft tissues of the body. It is also the anchorage for the muscles that enable the body, fins, jaw and many other dynamic elements to move.

In virtually all freshwater fish, this skeleton is formed of bone, and fish with bony skeletons are referred to as teleosts. This differentiates them from the marine sharks and rays, whose skeleton is made of cartilage. However, in a small number of freshwater fish, a portion of the skeleton is formed from cartilage. For example, in the African reedfish and bichirs, a portion of the skull is formed from cartilaginous material.

The structure of the skeleton
The skeleton can be crudely divided into three main sections: the backbone, the skull and the skeletal

supports for the fin rays. The backbone, or vertebral column, is made up of a series of individual bones connected by flexible ligaments that allow the backbone to flex, which is essential during swimming. It runs the length of the fish, from the rear of the head to the base of the tail. The ribs, suspended from the mid-zone of the vertebral column, surround and protect the vital organs in the body cavity. Along the upper edge of the vertebrae are the neural spines, one per vertebra, through which the spinal cord passes.

At the front end of the vertebral column is the skull, a series of fused or connected smaller bones, which together house the brain, eyes and other sense organs and provide a support for the jaw and gill arches. The skeletal supports for the fin rays arise from the backbone and skull.

Where muscle joins the skeleton
It is usually, though not always, the case that where muscle is attached to the skeleton, the bone in that area is thickened and enlarged. This is particularly true where there is a heavy dependency on muscle strength, for instance at the base of

Below: These Calamiana *gobies have a very wide gape, but this is not usual. It is the result of a protrusile jaw mechanism, whereby the upper jaw slides forward and the lower jaw articulates in response.*

the tail (the prime-moving element of most fish), and the jaws. Some species rely on locking fin spines for defensive purposes and strong muscular control is essential for these to work (see page 38). As a result, the muscle attachment points are significantly strengthened to handle the forces needed in effecting a lock. Examples of this can be found in many catfish, where the pelvic girdle, to which the strong pectoral muscles are attached, is particularly heavily built. (The pelvic girdle, or the 'breast bones', on the underside unite the two sides between the bases of the pectoral fin spines.)

The bony structure of the skeleton has a higher specific gravity than water, giving the fish ballast in the water and a tendency to sink. This is countered by the buoyancy of fat and the gas contents of the swimbladder,

which allow it to control its depth in the water column (see pages 58-59 for how the swimbladder works).

The muscles
The bulk of the body is composed of muscle. The lateral bands that cover the flanks all the way to the tail are the most important group, as these are the muscles used for swimming. Each muscle segment is roughly S-shaped and these muscle bands, or myotomes, correspond in number to the vertebrae. The myotomes are also divided into an upper and lower section. If you have ever taken the skin off a piece of fish (cooked or raw) you can see that the flesh has a zigzag pattern. The lighter zigzag lines are the myocommata, thin partitions between each of the myotomes. Thousands of tiny muscle fibres run between, and are attached

Right: *Looking at the transparent body of the glass catfish, you can clearly see the soft organs and swim-bladder located in the forward part of the fish. Because these are more buoyant than the skeleton (of which the centre of gravity is further back) the glass catfish holds itself at an angle when at rest.*

Below: *On some naked (scaleless) fish, such as this juvenile clarias catfish, it is possible to see the zigzag outline of the muscle segments along the body.*

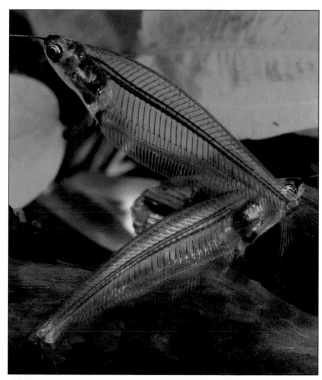

to these thin partitions. The action of the muscles contracting and relaxing on either side of the vertebral column throws the body into a series of curves that start at the head and progress to the tail. These swing the body from side to side in a series of sinuous curves, effectively propelling the fish forward.

Around the head and fins, the mytomes may be modified to cope with more specific movements, such as locking the fin spines, opening the jaws and moving the eyes.

Red and white muscle

Fish have two forms of muscle: red and white. Red muscle has a good blood supply and contains myoglobin (an oxygen-carrying chemical similar to the haemoglobin found in blood) and a reasonable amount of fat. White muscles have a poor blood supply, no myoglobin and little fat. The red muscle forms a thin layer on the outside of the main white muscle mass and is used primarily for more constant swimming, whereas the white muscle mass is used for sudden bursts of speed or other activity. This means that fish that lurk and make rapid movements to catch prey have little red muscle, while those that cruise the rivers and lakes have more red muscle.

The blood system

The most important part of the blood system is the heart. In bony fish, it is a simple, small, muscular organ, usually found just below the pharynx and right behind the gills.

The heart is in four parts: a chamber, the sinus venosus, that receives the blood from the veins; an atrium or auricle; the ventricle, which

Blood circulation

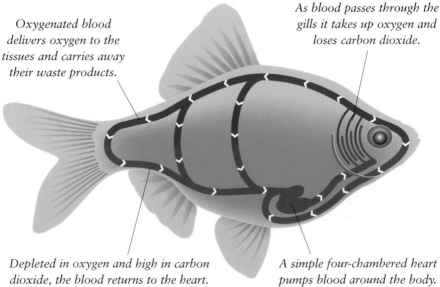

Oxygenated blood delivers oxygen to the tissues and carries away their waste products.

As blood passes through the gills it takes up oxygen and loses carbon dioxide.

Depleted in oxygen and high in carbon dioxide, the blood returns to the heart.

A simple four-chambered heart pumps blood around the body.

UNDER THE SKIN

has thick muscular walls used to pump the blood around the body; and, at the base of the main artery that carries blood to the gills, a bulb. In more primitive bony fish, this bulb is muscular and functions much like the ventricle, but in the higher bony fish it cannot contract. In lungfish, the auricle and ventricle are divided by a partition.

In general terms, blood passes out of the ventricle, through the bulb and into a main artery, the ventral aorta, that runs forwards in the lower part of the body. This has branches on either side that carry the blood to the gills, where respiratory gases are exchanged. Once depleted of its carbon dioxide and enriched by

Above: Fish propel themselves along by flexing the muscle segments and throwing the body into S-shaped curves, clearly demonstrated here by the tyre-track eel.

oxygen, the blood flows into a main artery, the dorsal aorta, in the upper part of the body. Branches off this main artery deliver the blood supply through successively smaller vessels to all parts of the fish. Once it has delivered its oxygen to the oxygen-depleted body cells, it takes up their waste products and returns to the heart through the veins. All the veins (except those from the liver and intestine) unite into two large veins that join and empty their contents into the sinus venosus.

Fish have far less blood in their system than higher vertebrates and its flow is a good deal slower. It is also colder, being only slightly higher (and sometimes lower) than the surrounding water temperature.

Fish also have a lymphatic system, a fine network of tubes found in the connective tissue of various parts of the body. Its purpose is to collect the blood plasma (the liquid part of blood without the red blood cells), which oozes through the fine capillaries and feeds the tissues, and return it to the veins.

The gills and respiratory system

Fish need oxygen to live. Respiration is the process by which oxygen is taken into the bloodstream and carbon dioxide, a waste product of metabolism, is removed. Fish blood contains red corpuscles, whose haemoglobin is able to take up oxygen and then release it to cells in the body and receive carbon dioxide in exchange. The main organs that a fish uses to complete this process are the gills. But, as we shall see, one or two other parts of a fish can also be used for respiration.

The gills are located beneath the gill cover, or operculum, in the pharynx, the chamber at the back of the mouth just in front of the narrow gullet. If you lift up the gill cover (do not try this on a live fish, as you can damage it) or try to look into the gill cavity of a large fish as it opens its gill cover, you will see a red mass of filaments attached to each of the gill arches. There are four gill arches on

External gills

In their early stages, the young of some fishes, notably the African and South American lungfish and the bichirs *(Protopterus)*, have external gills. The young bichirs have a single external gill that resembles a leaf on each side of the head, just above the gill opening. Young lungfish have four smaller structures on each side of the head. As the fully functional internal gills develop, so the external structures recede and finally disappear. However, in one or two species of lungfish vestigial remains can sometimes be seen.

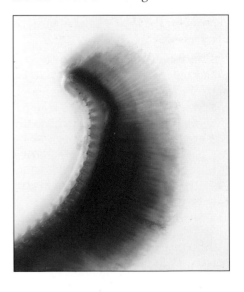

Above: *The red of the gill membranes is due to the blood vessels lying close to the membrane surface. A rich colour can be an indication of a fish's good health.*

How water is pumped through the gills

Water does not simply flow into the mouth and over the gills There is a coordinated series of contractions that create the flow.

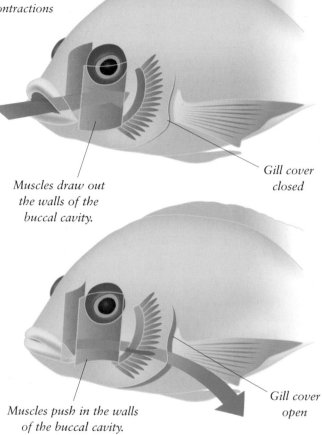

1 *Just before the fish opens its mouth the buccal cavity increases in volume, creating a negative pressure that sucks in water once the mouth opens.*

Muscles draw out the walls of the buccal cavity.

Gill cover closed

2 *When the fish closes its mouth, the water is slightly compressed in the buccal cavity. As the operculum, or gill cover, is opened, the water flows out, passing over the gills in the process.*

Muscles push in the walls of the buccal cavity.

Gill cover open

each side of the fish and two rows of filaments on each arch. Under magnification, they will stand out from the gill arch like a letter V. Further magnification reveals that the filaments are quite rough. Their surface appears to be covered in a series of folds that greatly increase the surface area in contact with the water, and thus the area over which gaseous exchange can take place. The actual surface area varies from species to species, but generally speaking, more active species have a much greater surface area than sedentary species.

As water passes over the filaments, only a very fine membrane separates it from the blood, allowing gases to pass readily from one to the other. In the tiny capillaries of the gill filaments, the blood flow directed in

How the gills work

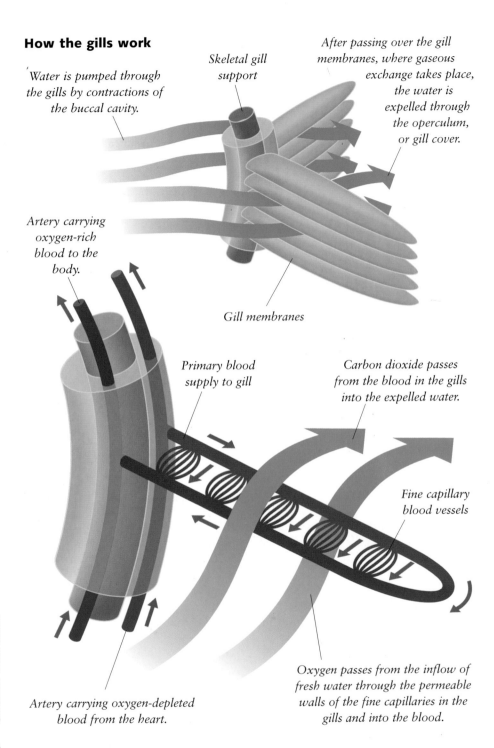

Water is pumped through the gills by contractions of the buccal cavity.

Skeletal gill support

After passing over the gill membranes, where gaseous exchange takes place, the water is expelled through the operculum, or gill cover.

Artery carrying oxygen-rich blood to the body.

Gill membranes

Primary blood supply to gill

Carbon dioxide passes from the blood in the gills into the expelled water.

Fine capillary blood vessels

Artery carrying oxygen-depleted blood from the heart.

Oxygen passes from the inflow of fresh water through the permeable walls of the fine capillaries in the gills and into the blood.

the opposite direction to the water flow. This ensures that they are in contact and able to exchange gases for as long as possible. Such is the efficiency of this countercurrent system that, under experimental conditions, absorption of oxygen was reduced from 50% to 9% when the direction of the water flow was reversed.

A slit on each side of the compartment housing the gills (the branchial chamber) allows water entering the mouth to pass to the outside. This opening is covered by the movable operculum. Water is drawn into the mouth and then passed back over the gills and out through the operculum by a pumping action. This can be clearly observed in aquarium fish by the carefully timed opening and closing of the mouth and operculum. Although it looks as though water flows through the system in pulses, it does not. In fact, the action of the mouth as a pump and the gill cavity as a second pump are slightly out of phase to ensure the continuous flow of water.

The gills play an important part in ridding the fish's system of some waste products, such as carbon dioxide, and 'poisonous' nitrogen-containing compounds, such as

The countercurrent system

To maximize oxygen extraction efficiency, water flows over the gills in the opposite direction to the blood flowing in the capillaries in the gill membranes.

The amount of oxygen in the water is always greater than that in the blood at any particular point. This gradient ensures that the blood continually absorbs oxygen in its passage through the gills.

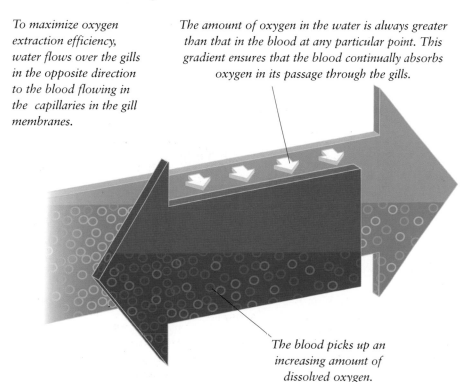

The blood picks up an increasing amount of dissolved oxygen.

ammonia and urea. Some cells in the filaments are also capable of taking up and excreting chlorides, an extremely important function in maintaining the fish's salt balance (see page 54).

Breathing rates

Fish can alter their breathing rate in line with their oxygen requirements. When they are at rest their breathing slows, but increases when they are active. If the oxygen content of the water is reduced for any reason, the fish will increase its breathing rate, as it has to work harder to get enough oxygen from the water. Temperature can also play a part in respiratory rates, but this is probably due to its effect on the oxygen-holding capacity of the water. Cool water can hold more oxygen than warm water.

The gill rakers

Filter-feeding fish need to ensure that their delicate gill filaments are not damaged or clogged by anything contained in the water as it passes over them. Gill rakers help to prevent this. Their purpose is to strain the water and prevent any solid particles reaching the gill filaments. These structures look like a double row of short, stiff rods on the inner edge of each gill arch, and stick out across the pharyngeal opening. The rows of rakers usually interlock and together they make a very efficient strainer.

A fish out of water

As a general rule, fish with large gill apertures die more quickly out of water than those with smaller ones. Fish suffocate in air, which sounds illogical when you consider that air contains more oxygen than water. However, in air the gill filaments are

Below: With its mouth wide open, the gill arches of this Batrachus are visible. The thorny-looking edges are the gill rakers, a filtering device that prevents ingested debris and food damaging the delicate gills that lie behind them.

Above: *Despite sucking itself to a surface, this* Panaque *is still respiring. It achieves this by taking in a small quantity of water through a channel in the suction lips. A pressure gradient maintains the suction effect and, as the fish is at rest, only small quantities of water are required for respiration.*

unsupported and collapse on each other, thus reducing the surface available for respiration. In addition, there is no water surrounding the filaments, which is necessary for any exchange of gases to take place.

The fish that do survive out of water have small gill cavity openings and the structure of their gills is different in that they are less likely to collapse when not surrounded by water.

Many embryo and larval fish can breathe through their skin. The medium fin fold is copiously supplied with blood vessels and acts as a gill until the true gills form.

The mudskipper can retain water in its branchial chamber so that respiration continues while the fish is out of water. However, the fish must keep returning to take gulps of water to ensure that the branchial chamber remains moist. This is especially important after it has been feeding on land.

Some of the catfishes and loaches are able to use their intestine for breathing, with the fish going to the surface to take in air. Excess gases are expelled through the vent. Some groups of fishes have developed accessory breathing organs (see page 95).

Water and salt balance

Freshwater fish have a much higher salt content in their body tissues than is present in the surrounding water. By the natural process of osmosis that takes place through the permeable surfaces of the body, such as the gills, they take in water and

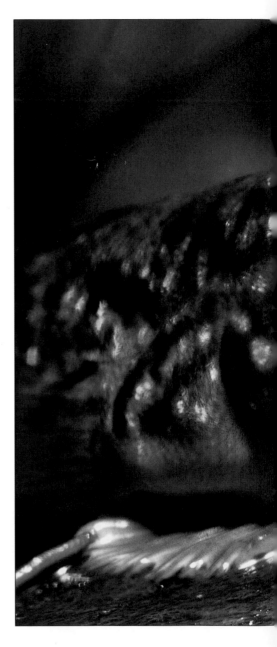

Above: The mudskipper (Periophthalmus barbarus) *spends a considerable time just out of the water. To make this possible, it retains some water in its mouth, both for* respiration and to prevent the collapse of the gill filaments. It must replenish its store of water frequently and returns beneath the surface for that purpose.

lose some salts all the time. Without a suitable response by the fish, its tissues would become saturated with water and deficient in salts. Freshwater fish excrete the excess water as urine, but they must be careful not to excrete too many salts. It is here that the kidneys play a vital role. Their function is to retain the body salts, while removing excess water from the blood that passes through them, and to excrete water as very dilute urine produced in copious amounts. The urine also contains urea, a nitrogen-containing waste produce of digestion. Urea is also excreted through the gills. Retention of urea would prove fatal to the fish.

Water and salt balance is also influenced by the thyroid and interenal glands. These are part of the endocrine system, other glands of which control blood pressure and are

Water regulation in freshwater fish

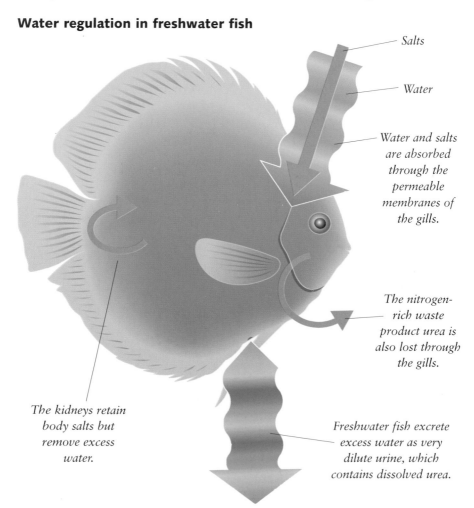

Salts

Water

Water and salts are absorbed through the permeable membranes of the gills.

The nitrogen-rich waste product urea is also lost through the gills.

The kidneys retain body salts but remove excess water.

Freshwater fish excrete excess water as very dilute urine, which contains dissolved urea.

Right: Some fish, such as the Monodactylus argenteus *shown here, migrate between marine and brackish waters and sometimes enter fresh water. To cope with these changing conditions, they 'reverse' the action of the system that controls water and salt balance.*

involved in colour change and calcium take-up. The endocrine system is governed by the pituitary gland in the brain, which is itself directly involved in sexual maturation and the metabolism of carbohydrates and proteins.

The swimbladder

The swimbladder is an adaptable organ; in some fish it plays a part in respiration, in others it is involved in sound production (see page 91) and hearing (see page 74). In most of the bony fishes, however, it acts as a hydrostatic organ, or float, that enables the fish to remain at any depth without rising or falling in the water column. To arrive at such a state, the density of the fish and that of the surrounding water must be just about equal. To achieve this in freshwater fish, the swimbladder needs to occupy 7-8% of the body volume.

The swimbladder is shaped like an elongated ellipse and is situated in the upper part of the body cavity, just below the backbone and the kidneys.

The swimbladder develops from the digestive canal and is connected by a duct to the foregut. In some fish this duct closes early on in the fish's development, while in others, including most freshwater fish, it remains open.

There is an ample blood supply to the swimbladder. In fish with a closed duct, the blood vessels are concentrated in an area known as the red-body, or gas gland, and it is through this that gases are secreted into the swimbladder. There is also a small, oval, highly vascularised area to the rear of the bladder, which can be shut off from the main cavity by a strong muscle. Its function is to remove gas from the swimbladder. A variation on this occurs in some fish in which gas resorption occurs in the rear part of the swimbladder, which is separated from the front section (where gas is secreted) by a diaphragm.

Those fish in which the duct remains open fill their swimbladder by gulping in air at the water surface. The bubbles are then forced down a pneumatic duct into the swimbladder. In the cyprinids, there is a bulb on the pneumatic duct that helps to pump the air down into the swimbladder.

For the swimbladder to function as a hydrostatic organ, a fish must be able to control the volume of gas inside it. When a fish swims downwards, external water pressure increases, so the fish must increase the volume of its swimbladder to maintain station in the water column. The reverse process occurs as the fish rises in the water column.

As may be expected, the gases found in the swimbladder are similar to those found in air – oxygen, carbon dioxide and nitrogen – but the proportions of each may differ markedly. Freshwater fish generally have less oxygen than their marine cousins, and in deep water freshwater fish species, the nitrogen content may be a high as 94%.

Not all bony fish have a swimbladder. For example, in bottom-dwelling species or even those that inhabit very fast-flowing waters, where the fish dash from one rock to the next, the swimbladder may be absent or greatly reduced. This makes complete sense for fish that live on the substrate or have little need to swim actively in the water for any length of time.

Usually located just below the vertebral column, the swimbladder forms a centre of buoyancy and its position can determine whether the fish adopts a head-down, head-up or horizontal pose when at rest.

Open swimbladder

In most freshwater fish the swimbladder has an open duct to the gut.

Closed swimbladder

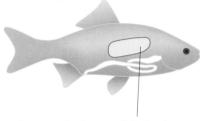

In some freshwater fish the duct closes off and the fish matures.

How a closed swimbladder works

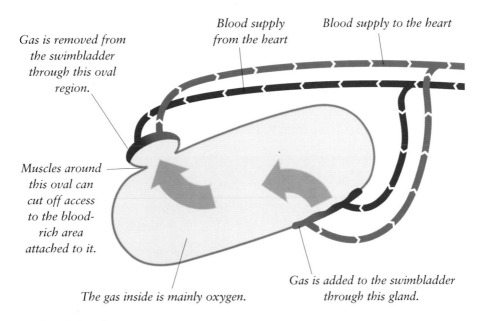

Gas is removed from the swimbladder through this oval region.

Blood supply from the heart

Blood supply to the heart

Muscles around this oval can cut off access to the blood-rich area attached to it.

The gas inside is mainly oxygen.

Gas is added to the swimbladder through this gland.

Maintaining buoyancy

As a fish rises to the surface it needs less gas in the swimbladder to remain neutrally buoyant.

Gas is resorbed into the blood here.

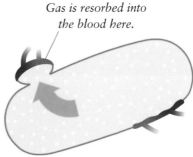

A constrictor muscle seals off this area to prevent gas diffusing into the blood capillaries.

As a fish goes deeper it needs more gas in the swimbladder to remain neutrally buoyant.

Gas is secreted into the swimbladder.

THE SENSES

All living creatures have senses and fish are no exception. The only difference is that they use them in water. It is easy to observe a fish's external features, but for a complete picture we must also understand the organs we cannot see.

Sense organs on display

On this African reedfish (*Erpetoichthys calabaricus*) you can see the inhalent nostrils for smell, eyes for sight and sensory pits on the head.

As you observe fish in the aquarium, it is obvious that they swim around avoiding each other and everything in the tank, but how do they do it? Some fish have only limited sight, so what sense takes over? How can a fish with eyes on top of its head hope to find food on the substrate? These are just three questions, and most fishkeepers can come up with hundreds more. If we understand how a fish uses each of its senses, we can better understand the way in which it lives and, therefore, how to care for it in captivity. And in any case, although it may seem initially complex, the subject is fascinating in its own right and an area that is often overlooked in books aimed at the hobbyist. The best place to start is the neural system, which gathers the information from each of the sense organs, passes it to the brain and sends a signal back in response.

The neural system

In its simplest form, the neural system consists of the brain attached to the spinal cord, from which nerve fibres extend. Messages pass to and from the brain through this network. As information is received from the various sense organs, such as those that provide vision, taste and tactile sensations, the brain analyzes the details and transmits instructions for any necessary action, such as swimming or eating, to the respective muscles or organs. The brain of a fish is similar in function to that of higher animals, including humans, but not so highly developed.

Perhaps the best way to understand the neural system of a fish is to compare it to the electronic systems of most modern cars. These are fitted with an electronic chip that processes information received from various sensors, and passes commands to the respective display and control devices for action. For example, a sensor may send a message to the chip along a wire that is an individual cable within a group of cables (generally referred to as a wiring loom) advising that oil pressure is too low. The chip will respond by sending a message, again along a wire that forms part of the wiring loom, to an indicator lamp to alert the driver.

The electronic chip is the equivalent of the brain, which is a wonderful organic computer; the wiring loom corresponds to the spinal chord, and the individual wires coming from the loom are analogous to the nerve fibres.

The brain is located inside the skull and forms an enlarged part of the front end of the spinal chord. The spinal chord passes through a channel in the vertebrae, continuing to the tail. From the spinal column, numerous nerve fibres, like individual

The brain and spinal cord

Encased in the backbone, the spinal cord runs the length of the body.

In this almost transparent fish you can see the large optic lobes of the brain through the thin skull bones.

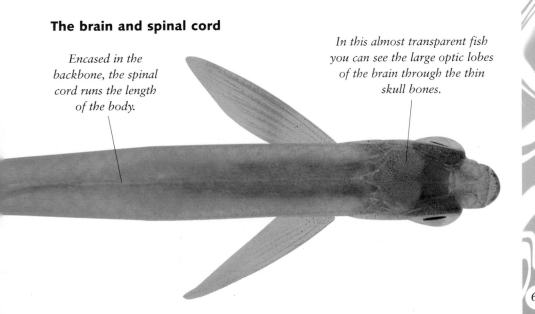

wires, are connected at their far ends to the various sensory organs, muscle blocks, tissues and other systems.

The sense of smell

It is true that fish do not have a nose and you might assume, therefore, that they cannot smell. However, while they may not have a nose, they do have nostrils, and there may be either one or two on each side of the head, depending on species. Two is the more common, but cichlids and other fishes in the perciformes (the perches and perchlike fishes) have only a single opening on each side of the head. Nostrils are generally located just above the mouth.

The nostril is a hole that allows entry to hollow lobes lined with

How the nostrils work

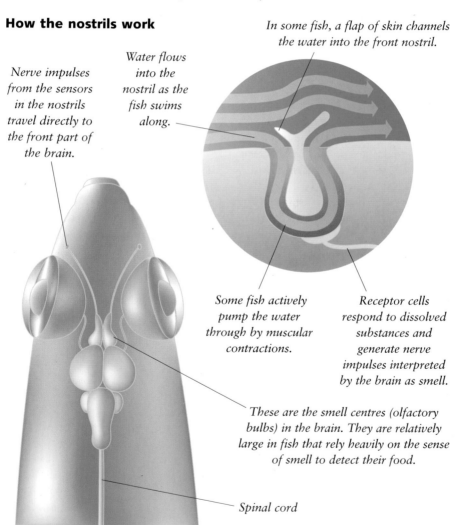

In some fish, a flap of skin channels the water into the front nostril.

Nerve impulses from the sensors in the nostrils travel directly to the front part of the brain.

Water flows into the nostril as the fish swims along.

Some fish actively pump the water through by muscular contractions.

Receptor cells respond to dissolved substances and generate nerve impulses interpreted by the brain as smell.

These are the smell centres (olfactory bulbs) in the brain. They are relatively large in fish that rely heavily on the sense of smell to detect their food.

Spinal cord

sensory receptors. The lobes are connected to the frontal part of the brain and provide the fish with an acute perception of smell.

In paired nostrils, the front and rear openings are connected. Water enters the anterior nostril, either in reaction to the current or pumped by muscles within the linking chamber, and then passes out through the rear opening. Sensory receptors sample the water as it flows by and feed information to the brain.

Fish with a single nostril on each side of the head inhale and exhale water through the same opening, pumping water by muscular action.

How much can fish smell?

The degree to which fish are able to smell varies from one species to another, and depends largely on the number of sensory receptors in the nostrils. These receptors are arranged on the surface of rosettelike, minutely

Above: Just in front of the eye on each side are the nostrils. Water enters the front hole, passes over olfactory sensory cells and exits through the rear aperture.

convoluted tissue clusters on the wall lining of the lobes. The greater the number of rosettes, the larger the area for receptors, and hence a greater perception of smell.

It is often the case that predatory fish have a high degree of smell, although this does not mean that all predators have a better sense of smell than other fish. Fish that live much of their life in murky waters depend less on sight than on taste and smell. Some small, omnivorous, bottom-dwelling catfish have twice the number of sensory rosettes (and by inference, twice the acuity of smell) than the highly predatory piranhas. This is often achieved by having a greater distance between the inhale and exhaust (front and rear) openings in which the receptors are placed. In some cases, the leading, or inhaling, nostril is fringed with a flap of skin or bone to 'scoop' in water.

The most important difference between terrestrial animals and fish is that fish only use the nostrils for smell, not for respiration.

The sense of taste

The major distinction between taste and smell is that smell can be perceived at a distance, whereas it is only possible to taste a substance by making intimate contact with it. In fish, the taste receptors perform more than the simple function of taste as we know it. They also register temperature fluctuations and touch,

although not in quite the same way as higher terrestrial vertebrates. They also respond to chemical reactions in the surrounding water, detecting the amount of dissolved oxygen or salts, for example.

Fish lack a tongue, but this does not mean that they have a poor sense of taste. Quite the opposite, in fact. There are many taste receptors on the inside of the mouth and around the lips, and often numerous sensors on the head and body.

Below: Many catfish, such as this Hemisorubim platyrhynchos, *use their mobile and highly sensitive mandibular barbels when hunting to locate prey accurately before lunging to feed.*

Above: The short barbels of the loaches lack the articulation of the mandibular barbels of some catfish. In loaches, the barbels only move in response to movements of the jaw.

Barbels – external tongues

Some fish, such as catfish and many cyprinids, have barbels. These filamentous appendages near the mouth could be loosely described as external 'tongues'. They are copiously covered in taste sensors.

With the exception of some catfishes, fish with barbels have little control of barbel movement. Mostly, this is confined to the actions of adjacent muscles at the barbel base, giving extremely limited motion. Many catfish, on the other hand, have a highly modified skull, in which one element of the jaw bones is modified as a basal part of the

main mandibular barbel near the corner of the mouth. In addition, muscles and surrounding skull bones give this mandibular barbel extreme articulation. This action is clear to anyone watching a catfish moving its main barbels, tasting the surrounding objects as it swims around the tank.

The form of barbels and their size varies immensely. In cyprinids, they are usually short and simple (not modified with branches or other refinements). However, on catfish and some other fish, the variation can be immense, even within the same family. Clearly, the more area over which the taste receptors are spread, the greater the ability to taste, offering a better chance of survival where nutrition is limited. Examples of barbel development include a membrane from the barbel to its base in *Hemisynodontis*

Above: The highly branched barbels of fish such as this Synodontis robertsi, *provide the fish with a large sensory area to seek for food. This is useful when you cannot see the substrate beneath you!*

membranaceus and branche barbels in many *Synodontis* species.

By moving their small mouths, some fish, such as the *Corydoras* group of catfish and the loaches, can shape their short, simple barbels into a funnel around the mouth, tasting food items immediately before ingesting them. In these fishes, barbel development can make up for poor visibility in the lower levels of the water column. Fish often use their barbels as they swim just off the substrate, trailing them across the surface in search of food.

Some anabantids have long, filamentous extensions to their ventral fins. These, too, have taste sensors. These fish inhabit mainly stagnant waters, and it is suggested that they use the sensors to detect areas of water with a richer supply of dissolved oxygen. The same function may be true for the pimelodid catfish, *Pseudoplatystoma sturio*, which has immensely long barbels – about twice the length of the fish.

The sense of sight

While taste and smell play a significant part in the daily routine of most fish, sight is of some importance when it comes to avoiding predation. Under water, distances appear compressed. Notice, for example, how close the rear of your aquarium appears when it is filled with water. Similarly, observe the way a straight stick seems to be bent when partially submersed in a bucket of water. This happens because water has a higher refractive index (light-bending power) than air. Another characteristic of water is its ability to filter light. The greater the depth, the less light will penetrate. Fishes' eyes are modified to take all these factors into account. They are generally long-sighted, with accentuated forward vision.

How fish eyes work

Generally speaking, a fish eye is similar to our own. Very simply, a lens at the front projects an image onto a layer of light-sensitive cells on the retina, from which information is passed by the optic nerve to the brain. However, there are fundamental differences between the working of a fish and a human eye.

Terrestrial vertebrates are able to focus on objects at various distances, both near and far, which they achieve by altering the curvature of the lens through muscular action. In fish, the curvature of the lens remains constant; instead, its distance from the retina alters. This is similar to the method used to focus a camera, where the lens is racked to and fro.

In humans, the iris that surrounds the pupil contracts to control the brightness level reaching the retina, much like the iris on a camera lens. The iris of a bony fish does not contract to any great extent.

The image focused by the lens falls onto the retina at the back of the eye. This is made up of two principal forms of photoreceptor cells called rods and cones. Rods are highly responsive to light intensity, and give the fish a perception of light and dark. They are particularly useful in low-light conditions, such as murky or deep waters, where light has difficulty penetrating. Cones need higher light levels to work and respond to wavelength, enabling most fish to have colour vision, a very useful facility when you consider the role of colour in courtship and defence displays. The ratio of rods

Left: The staring eyes of a piranha clearly look like those of a predator. Large and positioned close to the front of the head, they enable the fish to judge distances accurately in their search for prey. Cones in the retina provide colour vision, a useful facility in the brightly lit shallows that piranha live in.

Inside a fish's eye

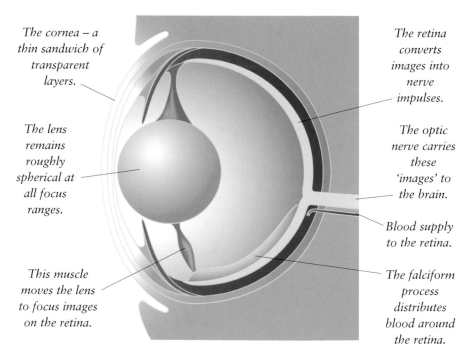

The cornea – a thin sandwich of transparent layers.

The lens remains roughly spherical at all focus ranges.

This muscle moves the lens to focus images on the retina.

The retina converts images into nerve impulses.

The optic nerve carries these 'images' to the brain.

Blood supply to the retina.

The falciform process distributes blood around the retina.

and cones in the eye of a fish vary considerably between the species, depending on need. For example, a nocturnal fish living in relatively clear water may have large eyes for collecting low levels of light, and an abundance of rods in the retina. On the other hand, a daytime-active fish living in brightly lit water can perceive colour because of the greater number of cones in its retina.

Clear, sharp focus is not achieved in the lateral vision of fish. This may help to explain why fish are easily misled by false eyespots or similar colour mimicry.

Fish lack eyelids. Their eyes are covered by transparent skin, and the outer surface is regularly cleaned by the constant washing of the surrounding water. Nor do fish have tear ducts, which also perform a cleansing task in humans.

The position of the eyes

In many fish the eyes are placed on either side of the head, giving them monocular vision. Because the visual fields of the eyes do not overlap, they see objects in two-dimensional, rather than stereoscopic, form and cannot determine distance. At first glance, this may appear to be a disadvantage, but fish with monocular vision and laterally placed eyes do enjoy virtually 360° vision in all planes. In addition, the movement of one eye is independent of the

What does a typical fish see?

*Most fish can see more clearly ahead
than to the side. To focus, the spherical
lens is moved to and fro in the direction
of the head and tail rather than in and
out of the eyeball. Because there is a
greater concentration of light-sensitive
cells on the retina nearest the tail, this
means that objects ahead can be brought
into sharp focus, while the less clear view
of objects at the side is not affected.*

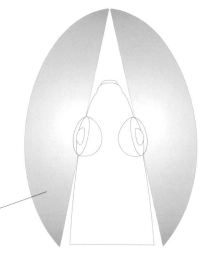

*The visual fields of these laterally
placed eyes cover a wide area but
do not overlap to provide a
stereoscopic view.*

*Objects in the forward
field of view are seen as
sharp images.*

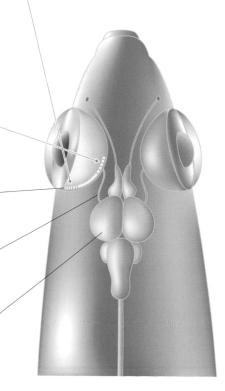

*Objects in the
lateral field of
view are not seen
in sharp focus.*

*In many fish there are
more light-sensitive cells
on the retina towards the
back of the eye.*

Optic nerve

*Optic lobe
of the brain*

other. (You can often see this in action when you observe a fish from the front.) Fish can thus detect any possible friend or foe, no matter from which direction it appears.

While many fish with laterally placed eyes can achieve a degree of stereoscopic vision at the expense of eye articulation, some species, mainly predators such as the pike characin (*Boulengerella*), have eyes placed closer together and facing forward. This allows them an acute perception of distance through stereoscopy, and is a useful tool for catching their next meal. The eyes can also be used independently, although all-round vision is more limited than in fish with monocular vision.

The position of the eyes often reflects a fish's lifestyle and the level in the water column where the fish spends most of its time. Most midwater fish, for example, have laterally spaced eyes, whereas some midwater predators have forward-facing eyes that provide a stereoscopic view. Bottom-dwelling fish, such as loaches and catfish, often have eyes placed towards the top of the head, as any unfriendly attack may well come from above.

Often, the eyes of bottom-dwellers will appear to be reflective and this is

Laterally placed eyes

Viewed from the front you can see that the fish is turning each eye to look forward, but the visual fields do not quite overlap.

Laterally placed eyes give good, all-round vision but do not provide a stereoscopic view.

Above: *The visual senses of the archerfish take into account the different refractive indexes of air and water, making its aim quite accurate as it spits water to 'shoot down' insects above the surface.*

the result of the high number of rods in the retina needed to see in the low-light conditions at the bottom of the water column. In some bony fish, 'eyeshine' may also be caused by reflective particles in the retina that 'bounce' the meagre amounts of light through the receptive cells more than once to improve sensitivity, although possibly at the expense of clarity. If these fish live in turbid or murky waters, they depend less on sight, and the eye is comparatively smaller.

Fish species that spend much of their life just below the water surface, such as some of the killifish, have eyes placed low down on the head. This is not the case for some surface-dwelling fish that take their prey from above the water. The archerfish (*Toxotes* sp.) spits water at insects above the surface, dislodging and devouring them as they fall into the water. The eyes of the archerfish are positioned towards the top of its head and are modified for aerial vision so that it can hit whatever it aims at. Even so, the archerfish is by no means always accurate when shooting for bugs.

Another surface-dwelling fish, the four-eyes (*Anableps* sp.) has eyes suited both for underwater and aerial vision. Each eye is split horizontally into two halves, the upper modified for aerial vision, the lower for seeing in water. The split in the eye lies conveniently at the water surface, as the four-eyes scours both submerged and terrestrial environments for food and possible danger.

Some bottom-dwelling catfish, such as many whiptails (*Loricaria* sp.), rely on a herbivorous diet. As their lifestyle suggests, their eyes are placed on top of the head, but they have a problem. They feed on algae, which requires bright light to grow, and being herbivores, they need to graze more-or-less continually. This means that the catfish must feed for much of the day in shallow water, where strong sunlight promotes lush algal growth. In these circumstances, the dorsally placed eyes are liable to

receive strong concentrations of light directly onto the delicate retina. To overcome this handicap, a flap protrudes from the top of each eye to act as a shade. This flap makes the eye look like the Greek letter omega.

Algal grazing is a drawn-out activity that often continues throughout twilight and sometimes into darkness. At this time, the fish require more acute low-light level vision, so the eye-shade flaps regress, and by night the eyes are more circular than omega-shaped. In captive whiptails, you can observe this by turning on the tank lights after two or more hours of darkness.

Hearing and balance

Behind the eyes of a bony fish lie the inner ears. These are not directly connected to the outside world, but form a complex series of three semicircular, hollow canals on either side of the head. Each canal is oriented in a different plane: one horizontal, one vertical and one lateral. Inside a swelling at one end of each canal there is a bundle of sensory hair cells with their tips embedded in a blob of jelly. These

Left: The flap over the top of this loricariid catfish's eye shades the delicate retina from intense sunlight as the fish grazes on algae. At night, the flap retracts and the eyes become more circular in shape.

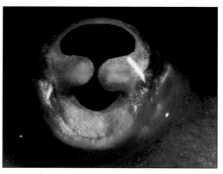

Above: The eye of the four-eyes (Anableps anableps) *is divided to give optimum focus both above and below the water surface.*

Right: This close-up view of the eye shows how it is divided to cope with life at the surface. Watching fish hunt live insects demonstrates the efficiency of the system.

Eyes for vision in air and water

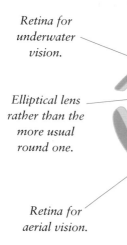

Retina for underwater vision.

Elliptical lens rather than the more usual round one.

Retina for aerial vision.

Light from above the water is focused through the short axis of the lens.

Water level

Light from below the water is focused through the long axis of the lens.

sensory cells respond to any movement of the fluid in the canals resulting from the yaw, pitch and rolling actions of the fish. They give the fish an appreciation of its attitude, or balance, in the water, so that the brain can send signals to various muscles to correct or adjust the fish's position accordingly.

In the lower part of the inner ear there are broader swellings filled with the same fluid and sensory cells, but here the cells are more spread out and respond to the movement of chalky deposits called otoliths. Vibrations passing though the surrounding tissue cause the otoliths to move and excite the sensory hair cells. This enables fish to hear.

In many freshwater fish, the inner ear is linked by a series of small bones to the swimbladder. Vibrations that reach the swimbladder through the body tissues are transmitted by way of these small bones directly to the inner ear. Not only does this amplify the signal, but also greatly improves the frequency range, thereby affording the fish an acute appreciation of auditory pitch. It also gives them a keener appreciation of the water depth.

How does a fish hear under water?

Most freshwater fish use the swimbladder as a 'collector' and 'amplifier' of underwater sounds.

Sound travels through water as a series of vibrations.

Otoliths ('ear stones') in the inner ear vibrate against hair cells that generate nerve impulses. These travel to the brain and are 'heard' as sound.

These linking bones transfer the sound vibrations to the inner ear.

The swimbladder vibrates in response to sound waves transmitted through the body tissues. The gas in the bladder amplifies the sound vibrations.

How does a fish keep its balance?

Like many other animals, fish have semicircular canals in the inner ear that are orientated so that they register movement in three directional planes.

This canal is positioned in a vertical plane from front to back. Movement of the fluid registers a pitching motion.

This canal is positioned in a vertical plane across the fish. Movement of the fluid registers a rolling motion.

This canal is positioned horizontally. Movement of the fluid registers a yawing motion.

Pitch *Roll* *Yaw*

How orientation signals are created

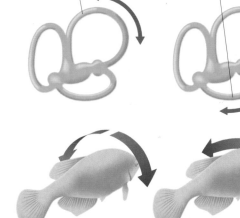

At one end of each semicircular canal there is an enlarged cavity containing a sensory organ that converts movement in the fluid into nerve impulses.

This gelatinous cap moves in response to surges in the surrounding fluid.

The hair cells protruding into the cap convert vibrations into nerve impulses.

Fluid-filled canal

Nerve fibres convey orientation impulses to the brain.

Underwater sound

Water is a good conductor of sound. Indeed, sound travels further in water than in air and five times faster. Underwater noise is actually quite rife (some say more intrusive than the 'muzak' that pervades modern life) and is mostly the result of water movement over the substrate, rocks and other obstacles. It can also be due to churning water at the surface in rapidly flowing water currents. Other sources of underwater noise include fish and other aquatic creatures, plus ships and boats.

The lateral line system

Other messages can also be received from the surrounding water, the main one being any pressure waves generated as water is deflected by nearby obstacles or other fish movement. The main sense organ for detecting this is the lateral line, which consists of a series of small pits down the flanks of the fish, starting near the back of the head and extending to the tail. Similar, but less uniformly distributed, pits can also be found on and around the head.

To understand how the lateral line system works, we need to review the hydrodynamic forces to which all fish are subjected. These are easier to understand if we think of them in terms of the dynamics of a moving car or an aeroplane passing through air. As the vehicle travels along, there is a higher air pressure on the leading edges, but as the air passes over the side surfaces, the pressure decreases. Manufacturers demonstrate this in wind tunnels using pressure sensors. Fish have to cope with the same type of forces and pressure changes, but for them they are exerted by water and not air.

Inside each sensory pit of the lateral line there is a small sensory organ known as a neuromast. The neuromasts are very similar to the sensory cells in the inner ear and are in effect biological pressure sensors that can bend through the influence of differential water pressure bearing

Right: The lateral line is visible as a continuous, or split, series of small pores along the flanks. Each pit houses a sensory organ, or neuromast.

How the lateral line system works

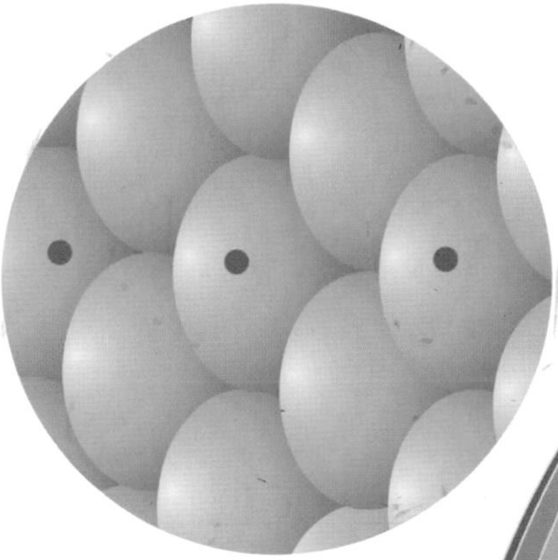

Left: Look closely at the flanks of a fish and you will see a line of pores running from head to tail. These are the openings to the lateral line, a sensory organ system that responds to pressure waves and gives the fish awareness of nearby objects.

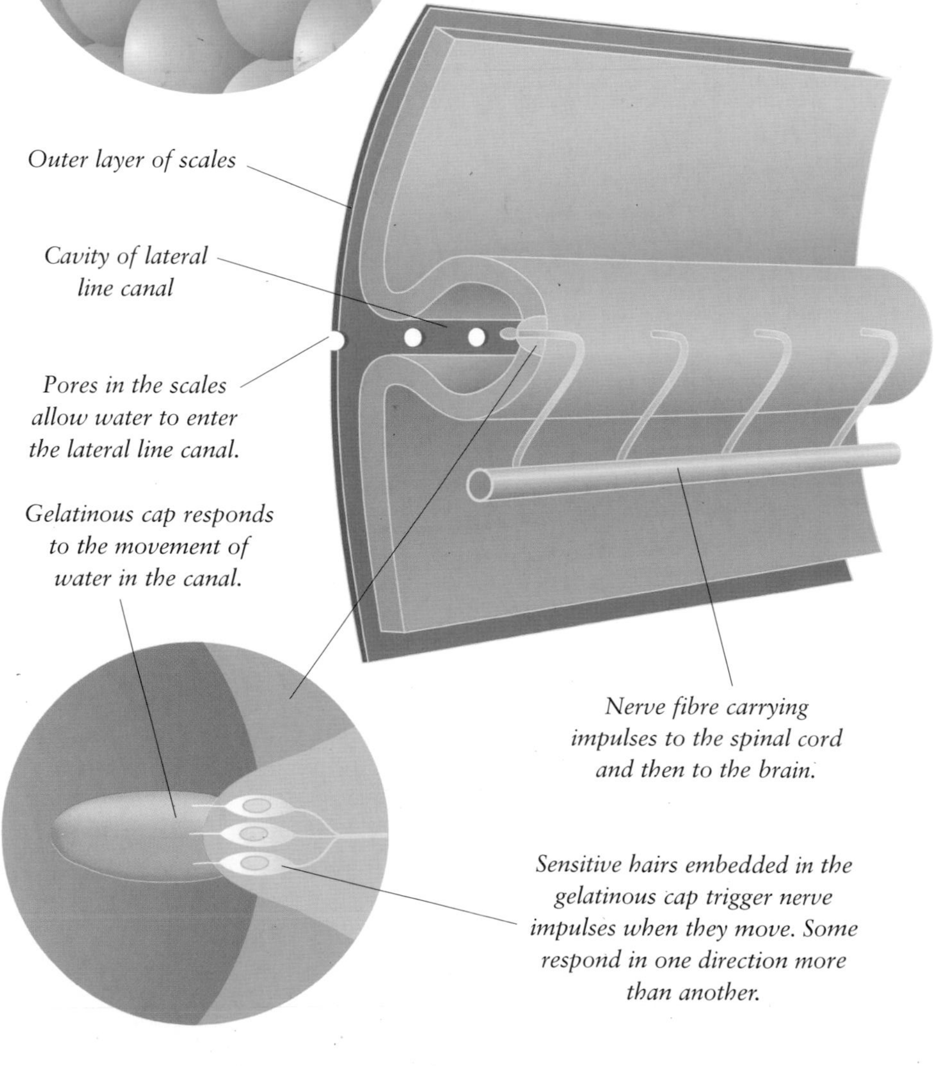

Outer layer of scales

Cavity of lateral line canal

Pores in the scales allow water to enter the lateral line canal.

Gelatinous cap responds to the movement of water in the canal.

Nerve fibre carrying impulses to the spinal cord and then to the brain.

Sensitive hairs embedded in the gelatinous cap trigger nerve impulses when they move. Some respond in one direction more than another.

Using an electrical field as a sense organ

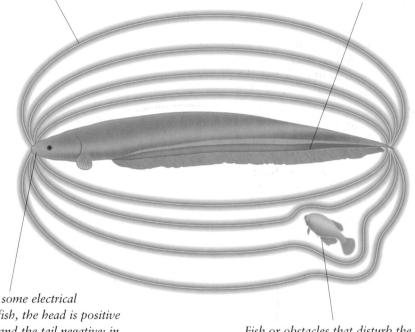

A very low electrical discharge from the electric organ produces a sensory field around the fish.

The electric organ in this Gymnotus *runs along the flank just above the long anal fin.*

In some electrical fish, the head is positive and the tail negative; in others, the polarity is reversed.

Fish or obstacles that disturb the field are registered as a change in its electrical resistance.

on them. This bending, its extent and direction, is picked up and transmitted to the brain by tiny nerve endings connected to the base of each neuromast. Signals recording differentials in water pressure received by the lateral line not only help the fish to detect obstacles and other fish, but also improves their ability to shoal.

Sensing by electricity

There are other ways in which fish sense their environment. Some,

though not all, are unique to fish and have developed as a result of the characteristics of water in which they live. One of these is the use of electricity as a form of radar.

Unlike air, water is a good conductor of electricity. Muscular movement involves the generation of minuscule electrical discharges. A small number of fish, mainly those from murky waters, have harnessed and fine tuned this electrical generation to create a weak field in the surrounding water. The electrical organs run the length of the body and create a field around the fish.

The fish instinctively 'knows' the electrical resistance of the water, but other obstacles, such as rocks, plants and even other fish, cause fluctuations or interruptions in the field and these can be detected by the fish. The amount of electrical resistance helps to identify the object, and the position in the electrical field defines its location. It has been discovered that when more than one of these fish are in close proximity to a member of the same species, the frequency of the electrical discharge from one will alter, so that it does not jam the signal from the other or cause any confusion to either fish.

Chemical signals

Fish are also known to emit chemical alarm substances to alert other creatures of impending danger, or chemical attractants to try to ensure that they find a mate to breed with.

Cave-dwelling fish

More than 40 species of fish live in caves in constant darkness. As a result, they lose the use of their eyes, although the eyes are present when the fish first hatches. However, as it grows, the skin thickens over the eye, making it appear that the eye is absent, whereas in fact it is regressed and can often respond to light, even though it cannot be used for sight. This is probably an energy efficiency measure in an environment low in available nutrients. Fuelling a function that has little use in constant darkness is a waste of resources.

Likewise, as vision is impracticable in the darkness of a cave, colour is also pointless. As a result, many cave-dwelling fish are unpigmented, appearing to have a pinkish hue, the result of the blood vessels lying close to the surface of the body. The blind cave-dwelling fish most familiar to fishkeepers is *Astyanax fasciatus mexicanus*, up to 9cm (3.5in) long.

As vision is of no use to cave fish, other senses are accentuated. This is demonstrated by their behaviour. Most 'blind' cave fish spend their time swimming close to a surface, be it the substrate or rocks and boulders, and rarely venture into midwaters. As they move, the feedback from the lateral line, in particular, but also from taste and smell sensors, gives them constant information about obstacles and nutrients nearby. It is as if the cave fish has the equivalent of a blind person's white stick to detect obstacles in their path.

It is interesting that in some species, notably *Garra barreami*, a cave-dwelling cyprinid from the Middle East, the optic nerves and optic lobes in the brain develop, as does pigmentation, when they are subjected to light. Whether or not this indicates a relatively recent evolutionary adaptation to this environment is not established. But it does show that when the need for a particular sense reasserts itself, it can be regenerated to a certain extent in some species. This goes against all recognized natural rules, which discount the possibility of brain regeneration.

HOW FISH FEED

The whole purpose of feeding is to ingest sufficient nutrients to maintain bodily functions. The types of food available are many and varied, and we often group fish by the type of food they eat or the way they eat it.

The position of the mouth is an indication of where in the water column a fish feeds. There are three principal positions. In the terminal position, both jaws are of equal length and at the front of the head. In the subterminal position, the mouth is on the lower surface of the head, with the longer upper jaw overhanging the lower. In the dorso-terminal position, the mouth is on top of the head and the lower jaw is longer than the upper one. However, that said, there are also many positions in between!

Life at the top

Hatchetfishes feed at the surface, either on insects that live there or fall onto the water. They can also 'jump up' to catch low-flying insects.

Surface-feeding fish

Fish that feed from the surface approach their prey from below, so an upturned (dorso-terminal) mouth is the norm. In captivity, these fish can sometimes be seen feeding in midwater, but they still approach the food from below. In extreme cases – maybe because they have been

Mouth positions

The shape, size and position of the mouth is a good indicator of how a fish feeds and what size food it can consume.

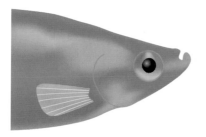

A longer lower jaw gives the mouth a distinctive shape and shows how the fish feeds by approaching food from beneath.

Terminal mouths are typical of midwater fish and allow the fish to approach their food head-on.

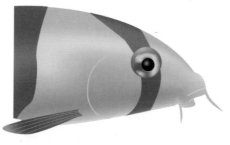

Extended upper jaws are seen on fish that approach food from above, such as bottom-dwellers feeding on the substrate.

offered the wrong sort of food – the fish feed from the substrate. To do this, they may turn on their side and flick up the food with their mouth, then quickly turn and take it from beneath before it sinks back to the bottom. A similar condition exists with bottom-dwelling predators, such as some of the gobies, who attack their prey from below.

Midwater-feeding fish

Fish with terminal mouths can take things from the surface and the substrate with equal ease. They feed mainly in midwater on aquatic invertebrates, other fish or on items that drift down in the water column or are stirred up from the substrate by themselves or other fish.

Bottom-feeding fish

Bottom-feeding fish that feed from the substrate have mouths on the underside of the head. These fish cannot see what they are eating, so barbels covered with taste receptors, or wide, fleshy lips also covered in taste receptors, help them to distinguish what is edible and its location on, or even in, the substrate.

Who eats what and how?

Where a fish feeds can also tell you a great deal about the type of food it eats. Surface-dwelling fish take creatures that either live at the water surface or fall onto it. Aquatic and terrestrial invertebrates and their larvae are primary sources of nutrients. Bottom-feeding fish use their barbels to detect food items in the substrate, including worms,

Above: *Fish are as safe as the size of their mouths! This is a good general rule, as fish with protrusile mouths can consume quite large prey in relation to their body size. This is Polycentrus schomburgkii.*

Below: *The delicate snout of the elephant nose has a small mouth at its tip. Bear this in mind if you keep this fish, because it eats small foods by grubbing in soft substrates and nooks and crannies.*

Protrusile mouths are typical of the perciformes, a group that includes cichlids. The ability to shoot the mouth forward gives the fish a better chance of catching prey because it does not have to approach too close to it. Many fish that lurk in the shadows to ambush a potential meal have this type of mouth structure so that they can lunge and grab their prey.

Why feed?

Fish may be described in terms of their eating habits – predators, algae eaters, suckermouths, etc. Some species may be omnivorous, eating items from various groupings. The barbs are typical in this respect, as they will grub in the substrate for invertebrates, feed on plant matter or debris, catch live food in midwater, take dead or dying insects from the surface, or a mixture of all of these.

Predators

In order to capture their prey, predators may have well-developed teeth to hold onto their prey and prevent its escape. Predatory fish have well-defined stomachs that produce very acidic secretions in order to digest their prey. Compared to that of a similar-sized herbivorous fish, their intestine is much shorter.

Predatory fish are not always active hunters; some species prefer to hide and dart out to capture passing prey, others actively hunt in a shoal, while another group will hunt alone.

The archerfish shoots down insects from overhanging vegetation. Good vision is of paramount

insects and their larvae, vegetable matter or dead animals.

Specialized feeders have mouths adapted to certain kinds of foods. For example, the long snouts of elephantnoses *(Gnathonemus petersi)* are designed to seek out small items of food in cracks and crevices or in very soft substrates. The mouth is located at the very end of this snout. It is small and can take only small prey items, such as aquatic worms. In total contrast, the very large and wide gape of the frogmouth catfish *(Chaca chaca)* is capable of engulfing an entire fish with room to spare! So, the size of the fish's gape can also be indicative of its diet.

The Mississippi paddlefish *(Polyodon spathula)* swims continuously with its large mouth open. It is a filter-feeder that gorges itself on very small aquatic organisms trapped in its close-set gill rakers.

importance to this creature so that it can take aim at its target and spit the water jet accurately enough to dislodge an insect from its perch. However, not all predators rely on their eyes to find their prey. Nocturnal fish, and those that live in murky, turbid waters, make great use of their barbels to taste, touch and locate prey before they lunge to grab it. They employ their nostrils and lateral line to great effect to detect prey at a distance.

Plant eaters

The best-known grazing fish in the aquarium trade are probably the loricariid catfish. Most of these fish graze over algae-covered rocks and feed not only on the algae, but also on the microorganisms living in it.

Algae is not the only green food that plant eaters seek out. Aquatic

Above: Labeotropheus fuelleborni *has a fleshy snout that protects the underslung mouth as the fish grazes over rocks, eating algae and seeking out the microorganisms that form an important part of its diet.*

plants are also a good food source, and fish such as pacu and metynnis consume them with relish. Many fish also eat the fruits and seeds that fall into the water from overhanging trees and bushes. (Seeds that travel through the body and are passed out in the faeces, help to spread plant species to new areas.)

Plant eaters need to feed more often than flesh eaters, because plant material has a lower nutrient value. Herbivores graze almost continuously during the day; if you keep such fish, it is important that the right type of food is always available to them.

Mud grubbers

Many fish grub in the substrate to find food. Some have a sucker mouth on the underside of the head and, as they are unable to see what they are resting on, it is well provided with taste receptors to detect prey items in soft silt and mud. The fish take a mixture of mud and food into their mouths, where the food is separated out and swallowed. Unwanted silt is passed out through the gills. *Labeo* species are typical examples of fish using this feeding method.

Many omnivorous fish also feed by grubbing in the substrate, but their jaws can cope with coarse substrates such as sand and, depending on the size of the fish, coarse gravels. Whatever the form of the mouth, these fish eat insect larvae, aquatic worms and general detritus, such as plant debris and animal remains.

Specialist feeders

Just as fish species take advantage of every available habitat, so some take advantage of strange food sources. One fish eats the scales from the sides of fish, and another eats their fins. Some take chunks of flesh from

Below: The delicate, fimbriated barbels of synodontis catfishes are covered in taste receptors. These are vital to help them distinguish food items amid the silt and fine sand they sift through.

Above: Piscivores (fish-eaters), such as this Xenentodon cancila, *have jaws that bristle with sharp teeth. They enable the predator to catch and hold onto their slippery prey before turning it round headfirst and then swallowing it whole.*

other fish and one small parasitic catfish enters the gills of larger fish to feed on the rich blood supply. This type of parasitic feeding ensures that the host fish remains alive and well and able to provide the parasite with further meals. Such specialized dietary needs can be extremely difficult to cope with in the aquarium and alternative food sources may need to be found.

Sometimes, fishkeepers get it wrong when it comes to a fish's diet. For a long time, the Malawian eyebiter (*Dimidiochromis compressiceps*) was believed to feed on the eyes of other fish. However, observations in the Lake and in aquariums have shown that this fish simply feeds on other fish and the common name is misleading.

The teeth

Teeth develop from skin. They are formed of dentine, have a pulp-filled cavity in the centre and are coated with enamel. Since they develop from skin, they can be found just about anywhere in the mouth. In bony fish (as opposed to the sharks and rays, where teeth are only found in the jaws) teeth may be found in the throat, on the roof of the mouth or on the tongue. The teeth can be irregular or grow in rows along the jaws or in broad patches or bands. For the most part they are firmly attached, but in some instances they may be movable. In some characins, the teeth are implanted in sockets in the underlying bone. Replacement of teeth is irregular; new teeth may form below or inbetween the existing teeth. The shape and size of the teeth can vary greatly and are, of course, closely related to the fish's diet.

The jaw teeth

As their name suggests, the jaw teeth are found on the jaws and may take

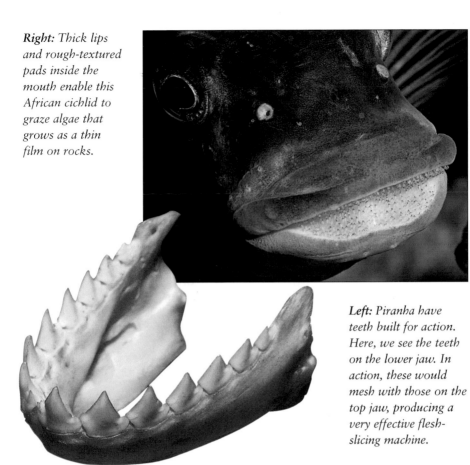

Right: Thick lips and rough-textured pads inside the mouth enable this African cichlid to graze algae that grows as a thin film on rocks.

Left: Piranha have teeth built for action. Here, we see the teeth on the lower jaw. In action, these would mesh with those on the top jaw, producing a very effective flesh-slicing machine.

various forms. Canine-like teeth are used for grasping and holding prey. They are strong and fanglike. Incisors have sharp edges and are used for cutting into flesh. Molars are flattened teeth used to crush and grind food. Some fish have very fine cardiform teeth. These consist of a band or patch of teeth that look like the tool used by spinners and weavers to card wool before it is spun into yarn, hence the name. Villiform teeth are slightly longer than cardiform teeth. Both types are used to hold prey in place and

prevent its escape.

Plankton feeders usually lack teeth, as do some of the more generalized omnivores.

Gill rakers

As well as protecting the delicate gill filaments from damage by coarse or abrasive food items, the gill rakers may be used when feeding. Most, but not all, plankton feeders have numerous elongated gill rakers with various appendages that allow microscopic plankton to be filtered out as water passes through the gills.

87

Once past the mouth...

Fish rarely choke on their food, although some fish predators that inadvertently try to swallow a stickleback or a spiny catfish may get the creature lodged in the throat. Generally speaking, the throat distends and allows the prey to pass through it, so much so that if a fish can fit the food into its mouth, it can usually swallow it. To make it easier to swallow, fish eaters (piscivores) generally engulf their prey headfirst to avoid any spines or scales becoming lodged in the throat. If they should catch their prey sideways on, they will usually try to turn the fish until it is pointing headfirst into the mouth.

The stomach

The stomach is the part of the digestive tract that secretes acid to break down the food. It has a different lining to the intestine.

In piscivores, the stomach is an elongated affair, while in omnivores it is more like the sac-shaped organ found in humans. In some fish, the stomach is a grinding organ, with highly thickened, muscular walls. It is not used so much for the initial digestion of food, but for grinding it up, much as a chicken grinds food in the gizzard.

One major adaptation of the stomach is seen in the pufferfishes, which can inflate and deflate their stomachs at will for defensive purposes.

Not all fish have a stomach. The type of food the fish eats is no indication of whether it has a stomach or not; rather, it is the size of the food particles it ingests or its ability to break up or grind food into suitably sized particles that dictate whether a stomach is present.

The digestive process

The point of the digestive system is to break down food into a form that the body can absorb and use in the metabolic process. During the digestive process, it may also be possible to remove potentially dangerous or toxic substances from the food.

Food is moved through the digestive system by contractions of the muscles. In predatory fish, the long muscles in the wall of the oesophagus extend into the stomach and allow these fish to regurgitate food with ease. This action can often have dire consequences in captivity, as the acids released into the aquarium water can knock out the beneficial bacteria colonies in the filter systems, allowing the water to become foul.

The complete digestive tract is lined with a mucous membrane. There are no salivary glands to lubricate it and thus ease the passage of food. The thick mucus coating also protects the lining of the digestive tract, which is able to stretch considerably to allow large pieces of food to pass easily through the system. As the food passes through the system, enzymes are produced to break it down into a fairly fluid form. When it reaches the intestine, whose function is to complete digestion, fluids from the liver, gall bladder and pancreas flow in to aid the process.

The intestine

The intestine varies in length in fish of a comparable overall size, being shorter in carnivores and longer in herbivores. The walls of the intestine are increased in area by many folds of tissue, making it far more efficient at absorbing nutrients. Depending on the type of diet, the intestine may be straight, folded in one or two loops, or very long and coiled into many loops in order to maximize the absorptive area in the minimum amount of body cavity space.

In the majority of bony fish, the last part of the digestive tract is the large intestine, which leads directly to the outside, opening at the vent, or anus. This is usually found just in front of the urinary opening and the reproductive openings. The position of the vent can vary considerably. In its primitive form, it is found at the back end of the fish, but it may also be found between, or even in front of, the pectoral fins. In the electric eel (*Electrophorus* sp.), for example, it is located under the throat!

In lungfishes, the situation is slightly different. The vent opens into the cloaca, which also has the ducts from the kidneys and the reproductive organs opening into it.

The digestive system

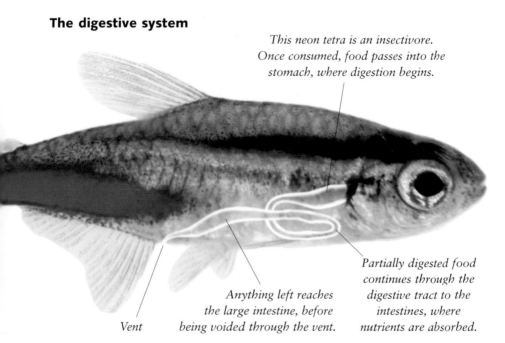

This neon tetra is an insectivore. Once consumed, food passes into the stomach, where digestion begins.

Anything left reaches the large intestine, before being voided through the vent.

Vent

Partially digested food continues through the digestive tract to the intestines, where nutrients are absorbed.

SPECIAL STRATEGIES

Some fish have developed specialized strategies to overcome the difficulties they encounter, and unusual methods of using unlikely resources. Making sounds, surviving drought and producing powerful electrical discharges are examples.

We have already examined how a fish hears (see page 74). If a fish can hear, then it is reasonable to assume that it can also produce sound. After all, water is such a good transmitter of sound that it would be an easy way to establish contact in murky water or, indeed, total darkness.

Making sounds the simple way
The simplest ways in which fish produce sound are by movements connected with swimming and by the release of gas from the swimbladder through the pneumatic duct. Many

A resourceful catfish

Clarias catfish are renowned both for their ability to breath air and for their migrations overland to seek new watercourses in times of drought.

of the hisses and grunts that fish emit when caught are made as gas from the swimbladder passes out of the mouth. Many cyprinids make noises in this way, but it is believed that the loaches make similar sounds by expelling air through the anus.

Another method of producing sound is by stridulation. The botias are well known for the clicking sounds they make when they are agitated, maybe a territorial dispute or simply someone trying to catch them. They achieve this noise by moving the bifid spine, which lies in a groove beneath the eye. Catfish also use stridulation to produce sound, and the pectoral, dorsal, anal or ventral fins may be involved. In the case of the pectoral fin, for example, the fish moves its fin spines and partially locks the ball and socket joint by tilting the leading edge of the pectoral spine downwards, so that it creates a grating, rasping type noise when the fin spine is moved horizontally. This is quite loud and easy to hear when catching the fish or when they are 'arguing' between themselves. Although it sounds quite aggressive, there is seldom any damage done.

The swimbladder as a sound organ

Sound production using the swimbladder is much more complex and involves muscles attached to the

Below: Doradid catfish produce sound in two ways: making a grating noise with their pectoral spines and a loud, booming sound by vibrating the swimbladder using an elastic spring mechanism.

swimbladder. When these are contracted and relaxed, they cause the swimbladder to vibrate. Generally speaking, sound produced by vibration of the swimbladder has a much lower frequency than that produced by stridulation.

Catfishes use an apparatus called the elastic spring mechanism to make the swimbladder vibrate. In these fish, the fourth vertebra is modified to produce two expanded disclike ends known as the 'springs'. The front of these springs is attached to the front part of the swimbladder. Two very strong muscles are attached to the back of the springs. The muscles run from there to the back of the skull, where they are firmly attached. When the muscles contract, they pull on the swimbladder and distort the walls, causing it to vibrate. The rapid vibrations set up a growling or humming sound,

amplified by the movement of the gases inside the bladder. Using this system, the intensity and pitch of a sound can vary from species to species. For example, the doradids produce a very low growling sound that can travel over great distances in water and can even be heard in the open air several metres away. The electric catfish, on the other hand, makes a much higher hissing sound.

Aestivation

When rivers, streams, lakes and pools dry up, most of the aquatic organisms die. However, it is well known that during periods of drought, some creatures, such as the

Below: African lungfish (Protopterus *spp.*) *aestivate in the wild. This survival tactic is like hibernation and is triggered by climatic conditions. It is not usually attempted by fish kept in captivity.*

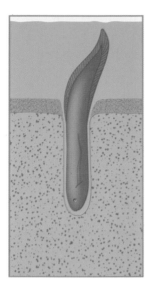
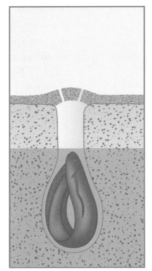
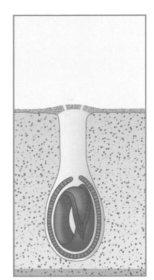

Above: The process of aestivation begins with the fish burrowing downwards into the substrate to make a chamber and concludes with the fish safely coiled in its cocoon for several months.

annual killifish and even tiny creatures such as daphnia, maintain the continuity of the species by producing drought-resistant eggs. The African lungfish *(Protopterus)*, however, uses another method: it aestivates in a secure cocoon.

As the water turns to a thick mud, the lungfish burrows head-down into the soft substrate, using its head and body to widen the burrow at the bottom. This allows it to turn back on itself until it rests in a coil. As the water level recedes, the lungfish secretes copious amounts of mucus that surrounds it and then hardens, encasing the fish in a cocoon. The only opening is where the mouth is. The air tube at the top of the cocoon

has a dried mud lid that allows air to percolate through to the fish so that it can breathe. Encased in its leathery cocoon and surrounded by rock-hard earth, the lungfish is able to survive the three to four month-long dry season. Should the rains fail, there are records of lungfish surviving until the following year.

During aestivation, the fish's metabolism slows right down, which also reduces its oxygen consumption considerably. In a normal dry season, a healthy fish has plenty of reserves – mostly muscle tissue – to maintain it, but if aestivation is extended for any reason, the fish may be very emaciated when it finally emerges. The fish is reawakened by the rains. Water fills the air tube, preventing air from reaching the fish's lungs (that is to say, it could drown) and the fish reacts by breaking the softening cocoon and resuming life in water using its gills.

93

Above: Anabantids, such as this dwarf gourami (Colisa lalia), *have an accessory breathing apparatus that allows them to take in air. This adaptation enables them to survive extreme conditions in the wild.*

Accessory breathing organ

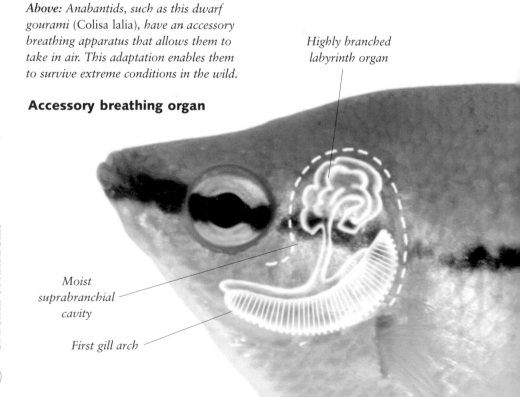

Highly branched labyrinth organ

Moist suprabranchial cavity

First gill arch

Air breathing

Fish that live in oxygen-deficient waters must swim to the surface to avoid suffocation. Many fish have developed a method of taking in bubbles of air to survive such periods, but in pools that are prone to drying up periodically or that become stagnant and foul because of dead and rotting vegetation, the ability to take in air at the water surface is crucial to the fish's survival. The anabantids have developed a labyrinth-like accessory breathing organ to cope with conditions in which the gills alone would be unable to supply enough oxygen for the fish's needs. It is from this organ that the anabantids have acquired their common name, the labyrinth fish.

The labyrinth organ is made up of outgrowths from the pharynx or the branchial (gill) chamber. These are filled with a spongy structure that has a large surface area richly supplied with blood vessels. Oxygen diffuses into these blood vessels from air stored in the labyrinth organ.

Some catfish, such as *Clarias* and *Heterobranchus*, have developed similar accessory breathing organs for precisely the same reasons. In these fish, the structures look like small, treelike growths on the upper ends of the gill arches. The growths are housed in a pair of chambers just above the gills. In *Heteropneustes*, the air chambers are similar to those of the clariids, but they form as long, tubular, lunglike structures that lie close to the backbone and extend from the branchial cavity to the tail.

The lining of the air cavities of *Heteropneustes* and the treelike structures of *Clarias* and *Heterobranchus* have a very fine structure, resembling that of the gill filaments.

Snakeheads are extremely tenacious of life, but their accessory breathing organ is a much simpler design compared to that of the anabantids and varies in its efficiency from species to species. The pair of cavities that perform the function contain no elaborate structures but are just lined with a thickened and wrinkled membrane well supplied with blood vessels. These lunglike chambers are pouches of the pharynx.

Some of the loaches and loricariid catfish also use their intestine to breathe. They have developed a method of taking in a gulp of air at the water surface and passing it down into a bulge in the intestine just behind the stomach. It is in this chamber that the oxygen is extracted by numerous tiny blood vessels that line the walls. The leftover gases are expelled through the vent.

Electricity as a weapon

As in all animals, minute electrical impulses are involved in the day-to-day workings of the nervous system in fish. Some fish have developed this capacity into a passive force for communication and navigation (see page 78), and some harness electrical power and use it as an active force for catching prey and deterring predators. This is not only somewhat amazing, it is also very efficient, because water is such a good conductor of electricity. Indeed, only creatures that live in water are able to take advantage of electricity in this manner.

In electric fish, the electric organs are made out of modified muscle tissue. When magnified, you can see that a typical organ is made up of a series of disclike muscle cells (electroplates) that are stacked up in a column, like a pile of coins. Attached to one surface of each of the plates are the nerve fibrils. The column of electroplates is embedded in a jellylike substance that is well supplied with blood vessels, and the whole thing is encased by connective tissue that gives it a tubelike appearance. Although the electrical potential of each electroplate is very small, it is possible to achieve a much higher voltage because the electroplates are 'wired' in series and the columns in parallel.

The best-known active producers of electricity are the electric eel (*Electrophorus*) from South America and the electric catfish (*Malapterurus*) of Africa. The potential of an adult electric eel is frightening; it can produce in excess of 500 volts – enough to stun a horse! Needless to say, these fish should carry a 'handle with care' label. Electric eels are often exhibited in public aquariums, where their electrical discharges are converted to light or sound. At rest the fish is inert, but when it starts to move, the smallest electric organ, the Sach's organ near the tail, starts to emit short pulses. The fish uses these to find its way around. However, if aggravated by an unwary aquarist or fellow aquatic creatures, it becomes very dangerous, and the two other electric organs (Hunter's and the main organ) discharge a powerful electric shock. Such is the size of the electric organs that they make up almost half the body mass. Polarity of the electricity is from head (positive) to tail (negative).

In the electric catfish, the electric organ is powerful and surrounds the

Left: The electric eel is a highly dangerous creature and should never be kept by the inexperienced aquarist. It has the capability to discharge over 500 volts to stun large prey including you! These creatures are best observed in the safety of a public aquarium.

Above: *In captivity, the electric catfish is an unassuming creature that spends most of its time resting among rocks and wood, where its drab coloration blends in with its surroundings. Only when searching for food will it emerge.*

Below: *Only by looking under the skin can we see why the electric catfish is so dangerous. An adult is a powerhouse that can deliver over 400 volts in its initial discharge.*

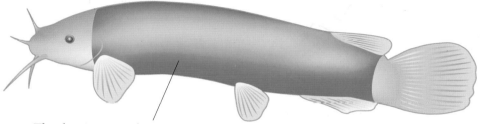

The electric organs form a protective jacket around the body.

Right: Heteropneustes fossilis, *a slim, slippery fish, looks unassuming, but treat it with respect when catching it or cleaning its aquarium. If you should be stabbed or scratched by the spines, painful wounds can result.*

body like a jacket. Its polarity is from tail (positive) to head (negative). Unlike the electric eel, it has only one electric organ, which it is able to discharge at will. The first pulse is the most powerful – in excess of 400 volts in an adult fish. Successive pulses diminish until the fish needs to build up its charge again. People have known about the electric catfish for centuries; it appears in Egyptian hieroglyphics dating back to 4000 B.C. Its electrical properties were also used by Arab and African peoples to cure illnesses – not something that should be tried by hobbyists or anyone else!

Venom as a form of defence

Fin spines are a very effective form of defence, but they can be enhanced by the development of poison glands at the base of the fin spine. Many species have them and they seem to

have only a defensive role; they are not used offensively to capture prey, as in, say, snakes. Their structure is relatively simple. They are usually formed from a group of specialized cells that seem to be the result of a modification of certain layers of the epidermis, which is part of the skin.

The stingrays are well known for the painful, and sometimes dangerous, wound they can inflict with the spines on their long tails. The groove that runs along either side of the serrated spine is a tract of glistening white tissue, usually hidden by the skin covering the spine. Its cells secrete the venom. The serrated spine causes a jagged, ripped wound, which allows the venom easy access into the host body.

Several of the catfishes, such as *Heteropneustes*, can inflict painful wounds with venomous spines. Some have smooth spines, others serrated

ones. In both cases, an epidermal layer covering the spines contains the glandular cells that produce the venom. These 'stings' can be extremely painful and may deaden the affected part of the body. Even a tiny prick from the spine of a small pimelodid catfish in the joint of a finger can cause painful swelling and immobility. Take great care when handling such fish. Immersing the affected limb in very hot water may provide some relief, but seek medical help if the pain and swelling persist; it helps if you can tell the doctor which kind of fish injured you!

Migration

There is a very fine line between the terms 'migration' and 'movement'. Both may be vertical, taking fish from a deeper level to the surface layers, or up and down a slope, such as the shore of a lake, or they may be horizontal. Horizontal migrations are better known, with fish travelling considerable distances, for example, from the oceans to freshwater to spawn, or from freshwater to marine waters to feed and mature.

Generally speaking, migration can be described as continuous movement with a purpose. It is totally under the control of the fish, being a genetically inbuilt system that is triggered by environmental factors, such as water depth, onset of the rains and pressure (both atmospheric and water). It can also be triggered by biological factors, such as sexual development, food and the fish's physiological clock.

Migration has a purpose, usually connected with feeding or breeding. Before setting off, the fish congregate and then travel together to the feeding or breeding grounds. Many migratory runs can be timed almost

Above: *Many of our aquarium fish, such as this* Leporinus fasciatus, *migrate in the wild. Depending on species they may be seasonal, in which case they are often long migrations, or diurnal (on a daily basis), which are shorter trips either along the substrate or up and down the water column.*

Right: *Snakeheads, such as this* Channa argus, *are able to migrate across land when weather conditions deteriorate. Such movements usually occur on damp nights, when they use their pectoral fins to haul themselves across the ground.*

to the day, and native fisherman take advantage of them to catch large numbers of quality fish.

In South America, some of the larger characins (for example, *Procheilodus, Myleus* and *Leporinus*) and catfishes (members of the Pimelodontidae) migrate upstream when the rivers Amazon and La Plata are in full flood. Some lake fish journey up feeder streams to spawn in the shallows. Other lake fish make vertical migrations each day to feed.

Triggering aquarium fish to spawn

In the aquarium, fish cannot migrate to spawn, so the fishkeeper must try to trigger them by making large water changes in an attempt to alter the temperature, oxygen levels, pH, hardness, etc. It may be a single factor that triggers the fish or a combination of several, but if you are lucky, you may hit on it.

'Walking' fish

Some of the strangest migrations are performed by clarias catfish, snakeheads and climbing perch. Should their river, stream or waterhole dry out, the fish 'walk' over land to try to find another water source. To do this, the clarias and snakeheads rise up on their pectoral fins and use them as limbs to haul themselves across the ground. These migrations usually take place on damp nights, when there is less chance of the fish becoming desiccated. The climbing perch *(Anabas)* also struggles across country to seek new waters, but this fish uses its gill covers as well as its fins to help it move over the ground.

REPRODUCTION

Without sex, species would become extinct. With it, they procreate and evolve. Captive breeding encourages the survival of fish species threatened by loss of habitat, etc., but first we must establish how they reproduce.

There are many species of fish living in a variety of habitats, so it should come as no surprise to discover that there is more than one way for fish to reproduce. Aquarists normally divide fish into two major groups: egglayers (oviparous) and livebearers (viviparous), and we will do more or less the same thing here. However, there comes a point where we may start to question when a fish ceases to be an egglayer and becomes a livebearer; in nature, boundaries are not so distinct and it is not always possible to give a definitive answer.

Good parents

Parental care among the cichlids is well known. This pair of *Thorichthys meeki* (firemouths) will defend their brood against allcomers.

Here we look only at freshwater tropical fish and some species that inhabit the brackish regions of the world. Amongst marine fishes, there are even more breeding strategies.

The reproduction organs
For fish to breed they need reproductive organs. In females, these

are the ovaries (hard roes) and in males, the testes (soft roes). In the majority of fish they are paired, elongate structures. The ovaries are located just behind the swimbladder (if the fish possesses one). They are pinkish yellow in colour and have a texture somewhat similar to compacted sand. When the female is ready to spawn, the ovaries become swollen with eggs. In the case of egglayers, to reach the outside the eggs must pass through the oviduct, which may have its own opening to the outside or may share the opening with the urinary tract. In the case of the livebearers, which produce live young, the eggs are retained within the body cavity.

The testes lie in a similar position in male fish. They are a good deal smaller than the ovaries, lighter in colour and have an almost creamy texture. Each testis has its own duct to transport the milt (sperm) to the genital aperture.

Not only do the ovaries and testes produce eggs and sperm respectively, they also produce sex hormones, which cause secondary sexual characteristics, such as breeding tubercles (a rash of spots covering some, or most of, the head) and flamboyant coloration in males. They also stimulate the sexual behaviour used in courtship and the maturation of the sex organs. The fish are then considered 'ripe', or ready to spawn. This way, none of the fish's energy is wasted in producing immature eggs and sperm.

Below: After spawning, the female medaka (Oryzias latipes) *retains the eggs close to her body until she passes through fine-leaved plants and brushes them off.*

Above: In certain species, the sexes look quite different. In this pair of killifish (Aphyosemion australe) *the brightly coloured, long-finned male is easily differentiated from the drab female.*

Differences in size, colour and fins

Secondary sexual characteristics are usually present during the whole of a fish's adult life, but may only become apparent when the fish is coming into spawning condition and disappear when it is over. They play no physical part in the mating of the two fish. The most obvious of these is the difference in size between males and females; usually the female is larger, both in length and girth. Depending on species, she may be five or six times larger than the male,

and in some of the livebearers, the difference in size is even greater.

Colour is another obvious difference. Once adult coloration has been attained it is always present, but will heighten as the breeding season approaches. Usually the males are the more colourful fish, for example, in rainbowfishes, killifishes and some of the smaller barbs, such as the cherry barb, the females look quite drab compared to males. In scientific circles, it is not unheard of for males to have been described as one species and females as another!

There can be differences in finnage between the sexes. For example, in some catfish, the first ray of the dorsal and pectoral fins is much thicker in males. The males in many cichlids and killifish develop long, filamentous extensions on some of the rays in the dorsal, anal and caudal fins. The fin membrane may also have distinctive eye-spots in various colours.

Very obvious fin developments are apparent in the livebearers. One example is the well-known 'sword' of the swordtail *(Xiphophorus helleri)*, where the lower rays of the caudal fin are extended. Another is the highly enlarged and brightly coloured dorsal fin of thc sailfin molly *(Poecilia latipinna)*.

Some fish show no easily distinguishable sexual characteristics; the only clue to the sexes is a deepening of the female's body, because her belly becomes distended with ripe eggs when she is ready to spawn. Such fish tend not to have

Above: The enlarged dorsal finnage and modification of the anal fin into a gonopodium of the male sailfin molly makes it easy to distinguish from the female, even at a relatively early age.

Exceptions to the rule

Some fish do not conform to the accepted male/female mode of reproduction. Sex reversal can occur and is known among the freshwater cyprinodonts.

The strangest anomaly is the condition found in the Amazon molly, *Poecilia formosa*. Naturally occurring all-female populations have been studied and found to reproduce. In other populations, fish have been found that look like males, but they have proved to be genetically 'female', and if they produced any sperm, it was unable to fertilize a

true female. Only a tiny minority of true males have been found in any population, so the part they play in reproduction is insignificant.

Although these mollies may seem to attempt to mate with similar species, in fact they never do so. The sperm from the second species stimulates the egg of the Amazon molly and it is this stimulation, and not the penetration of the sperm into the egg, that causes it to develop. This type of reproduction is known as gynogenesis and is also recorded in a wild population of the goldfish.

flamboyant courtship rituals. As a very general rule, if a fish performs a courtship display, the differences between the sexes is marked.

In some fish it is easy to see the differences, especially in coloration, with males in particular becoming much more intensely coloured. At such time he will not only be trying to attract a female, he will also be displaying to, and battling with, other males to defend a territory and prove himself the best possible suitor for any nearby females.

Changes in appearance at breeding
Subtle and not-so-subtle variations in different parts of the body also occur in some species. The bristlenose (*Ancistrus hoplogenys*), a member of the loricariid catfish family of South America, develops tubercles around its snout and these may extend up onto the head, hence the common name. When ready to breed these become more prominent and even the female may have some very short bristles around the very edge of her snout. With other species of loricariid, the shape of the snout may differ between the sexes. This is one characteristic that aquarists regularly use to sex whiptails; look down on the fish and you will see that the female has a rounded snout, while the male's is more pointed.

In other loricariids, males and females may have different-shaped mouths and lips, or in some, the interopercular spines just behind the gills may differ; ready-to-breed male loricariid catfishes have a full set of easy-to-see long spines.

At the onset of the breeding season, many male cyprinids develop tubercles on the head, which disappear soon afterwards. These are clearly visible on some of the barbs and may be mistaken for an outbreak of disease (usually whitespot) by an inexperienced aquarist.

A different protruberance that can occur on the head is the nuchal hump found on some cichlids. The mature males of some species have this all the time, but in other species, it appears when the fish is ready to breed and then disappears.

Genital papillae may also appear on some male fish. These short, brushlike appendages appear close to the vent of some cichlids and catfish. In the cichlids, they attract the mouthbrooding female to mouth at the vent, so that she takes in the male's milt to fertilize the eggs in her mouth. In other mouthbrooding species, the male has yellow 'egg-spots' on his anal fin. Once the female has collected the eggs in her mouth, the male spreads his anal fin, fooling the female into thinking she has missed some eggs. As she tries to pick up the false eggs, the male release his milt and she takes it in, fertilizing her eggs as she does so.

During the breeding season, the pelvic fins of *Lepidosiren* sp., the South American lungfish, appear bright red as the blood supply is increased to them. Why this should happen is not known.

It is worth noting that many of these sexual differences, especially fin shapes and colour, are characteristic of one species and as such are used

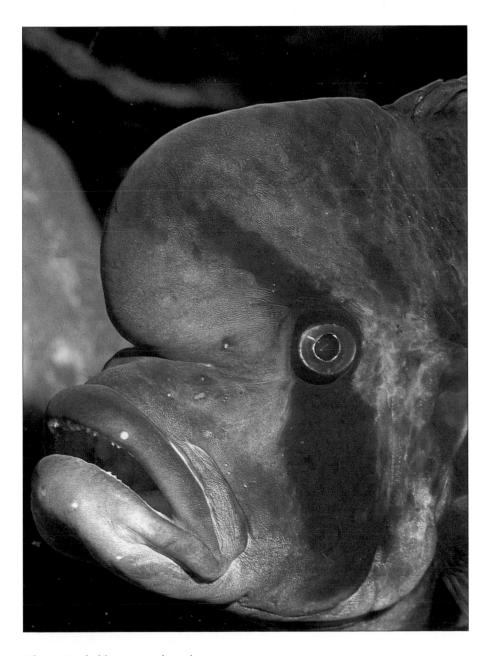

Above: *Nuchal humps, such as the one on this male* Cyphotilapia frontosa, *are seen on a number of cichlid species, but they are not always as prominent as shown here.*

as recognition signals, not just with regard to sex, but also to species identification, thereby reducing the likelihood of species crossbreeding. But even this is not foolproof and some naturally occurring hybrids have been recorded.

In nature, although the courtship displays of territorial fish that also build nests can appear very aggressive, it is seldom that any physical damage is done. Cichlids are noted for their displays, but one of the most pugnacious fish is the Siamese fighter (see page 116). Its threats and postures are usually sufficient to determine dominance. However, in the aquarium, things can change dramatically because we are inflicting the limitations of the size of the aquarium, coupled with a population density far in excess of that found in the same area/volume in the wild, and fights to the death do happen.

Courtship and spawning
Courtship can vary enormously from species to species, but the aim is the same: to encourage females to produce eggs and males to produce sperm. When the sperm and egg

Below: The threat postures adopted by male Betta splendens *may preface a full-scale fight between two males or, if the other male backs down, be a prelude to breeding with his chosen female.*

REPRODUCTION

Suspended animation

One group of fish worthy of mentioning are the annual killifish from Africa and South America. These spawn when the dry season starts, the pair diving down into the substrate, where they deposit and fertilize the eggs a few at a time. As the seasonal pools evaporate, the parents perish, but the eggs remain in the mud, protected by a drought-resistant membrane. As long as there is water in the pool, the embryos develop, but once it dries out, their development is arrested and does nor restart until the rains return. Hatching takes place shortly after this and the fry grow on to repeat the cycle the following year. Not all the eggs hatch at the first rains. This ensures that if the rains fail, some eggs remain ready to hatch when the floods return, thus ensuring the continuation of the species.

Left: The highly coloured male Nothobranchius *flamboyantly courts the drab but well-rounded female prior to spawning.*

come into contact, the sperm enters the egg and fertilization is complete. This happens externally with the majority of egglayers, and internally with livebearers.

The spawning season can be thought of as the time when the males and females have ripe eggs and sperm. This period can last for a few days, extend to a few months or be any time frame inbetween; it all depends on the species concerned.

The triggers for spawning are equally varied: the onset of the rains, a raising or lowering of water temperature, a raising or lowering of the acidity, alkalinity or hardness, variations in oxygen levels, light levels, increase in availability of food, or a combination of all these. And some species, for example some of the African cichlids, spawn throughout the year.

The egglayers

As you might expect, there are also many ways of egglaying. Some shoaling species gather in tight shoals and males and females release their eggs and sperm simultaneously so

Above: A spawning substrate does not have to be a hard rock or stone. The flat underside of a leaf is just right for this pair of Rasbora heteromorpha.

that they mix in the water and fertilization can occur. The eggs may be left to float free in the water or they may be scattered freely over roots and fine-leaved plants. Once the parents of these shoaling fish have produced a large number of fertilized eggs, they swim off and leave them to their fate. Some will be eaten by other fish, some will hatch, but relatively few will grow to mature adults. Other egg-scattering species may gather in a shoal, but a single pair will break away, spawn and then return to the shoal, while yet others just pair and spawn.

Some egglayers are depositors. This means that they place their eggs on a surface such as a leaf, a piece of wood, rock or a plant stem. Many then guard the eggs and subsequent offspring until they are of a suitable size to fend for themselves. Such species produce far fewer eggs than the eggscatterers, as egg and fry predation is much reduced by parental care.

Some egg depositors, such as some of the killifish and rainbowfishes, have no parental care. Rainbowfishes and some of the killifishes court each other and then dive through fine-leaved plants so that their adhesive eggs cling to the vegetation. This procedure continues over several days, with a few eggs produced each day until the female is spent. The eggs hang from the plant stems on long threads until they hatch.

With the killifish (sometimes referred to as egglaying cyprinodonts), the difference between the sexes is obvious, as the males are more highly coloured and have longer finnage. As they pair, the male

Right: Cherry barbs
(Barbus titteya) *are
shoaling fish, but a
pair will separate from
the shoal to deposit
their spawn among
fine-leaved plants. The
pair leave the eggs to
fend for themselves.*

Below: The bottom-
dwelling Brachygobius
*seeks out a secluded
area with a flat
substrate on which to
place its eggs. Being
defended by their
parents gives the eggs
more chance to survive.*

Left: To breed in the aquarium, splash tetras need broadleaved plants that overhang the tank. The pair will then leap from the tank, invert, and stick their eggs to a leaf.

Right: Mouthbrooders need only a small area on which to lay their eggs before collecting them for incubating. Clutches are relatively small; mouth size is the governing factor.

and female lie alongside each other and the male may wrap his dorsal and anal fins around her so that when their eggs and milt are released, almost simultaneously, there is a very good chance that the majority of the eggs will be fertilized.

For sheer agility in reproduction, the splash tetra has to be admired. This egg-depositor leaps from the water and the pair then invert and place their eggs and milt on the underside of an overhanging leaf. The male splashes the eggs occasionally to prevent them drying out. When the eggs have completed their development, they hatch and the fry fall back into the water.

The mouthbrooders

Mouthbrooding fish take guarding their young to an extreme. They take a small clutch of eggs into the mouth and incubate both the eggs and fry in the buccal cavity until the fry are large enough to fend for themselves. Depending on species, it may be the male or the female or even both parents that brood the eggs and fry. The length of time they brood the youngsters also varies from species to species.

The bubblenesters

The bubblenest builders construct a large nest of bubbles in which to place their eggs and fry. The well-known gouramis and some of the callichthyid catfish fall into this category. Anabantids and other bubblenest builders usually inhabit poorly oxygenated regions, and their foamy bubblenests keep their eggs and fry in an oxygen-rich environment. The male seeks out a very secluded, still, quiet area, usually among water plants that reach up to the water surface. Depending on species, he either finds a suitable floating leaf beneath which

to construct the nest or a tangle of plants that will hold the foamy mass together. To produce the bubbles, he takes a gulp of air and blows out mucus-coated bubbles that float upwards and are trapped by the foliage. Some species will even tear off pieces of plant leaves and stems and add them to the nest to help bind it together. Some species make small, ragged nests, while others

Below: After courtship, the male Macropodus chinensis *wraps himself around the female, their vents in close proximity. As they slowly tumble in the water, they release their eggs and milt.*

produce great mounds of bubbles that rise above the water surface. Needless to say, the bubbles will eventually burst, so the male must continue his activities if the nest is to survive long enough for him to rear the youngsters.

Once built, the male starts his courtship display beneath the nest. He will chivvy and cajole an interested, ripe female into swimming into his territory beneath the nest, where he will display until she submits to mating. The male wraps himself around the female, she expels some eggs and he, his milt. In some species, the eggs naturally float

upwards towards the nest, but in others, they fall slowly through the water column and the male breaks off his nuptial embrace to catch the eggs in his mouth before swimming up to blow them into the nest.

When spawning is complete – and it may take quite some time – the spent female retires to a quiet region out of the way of the male, who now takes on guard duties. He will take care of the eggs, fry and nest,

Above: When spawning is complete, the male Macropodus chinensis *takes on the parental role of guarding the eggs and subsequent fry. He keeps the nest intact until the fry are free-swimming.*

replacing any eggs and fry that may fall out and replenishing the bubbles as necessary. He is also quite merciless in chasing off would-be egg or fry predators from the vicinity. If you really want to see this display at its best, watch a pair of Siamese fighters *(Betta splendens)*. The male will spread his fins and flare his gill covers, shaking and posturing for all he is worth. But, do take care, because if the female is unwilling or not ready to spawn, his advances will turn to hate and he will attack her, biting and ripping her fins. Sometimes there seems to be a very fine line before love and hate in the fish world.

Territorial behaviour

Territorial behaviour can be quite dramatic, and the cichlids are probably the best group of fish to watch to study territorial behaviour. However, it is important to appreciate that what happens in the restricted area of an aquarium is not always the same as proceedings in the wild. Some fish dig large nests, their edges defined by a ring of debris they have excavated from the centre.

Above: For some fish, such as these cichlids in Lake Malawi, establishing a territory is an important part of reproduction. The size of any territory varies from species to species.

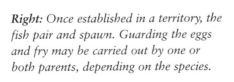

Right: Once established in a territory, the fish pair and spawn. Guarding the eggs and fry may be carried out by one or both parents, depending on the species.

This will be the spawning pit, but the fish's territory (depending on the size of the species concerned) may extend 1m (39in) or more all around the nest area.

The harem breeders allow several females into their overall territory and will breed with each of them. As you can imagine, this is quite a task and the male needs to be extremely fit and healthy to do this. Other fish defend a hollow in a log or under a stone against allcomers. In some species, the male guards the entrance of a cave and the surrounding area once the female is safely inside. In others, the female is chased off after spawning and it is the male who tends the eggs and subsequent fry. Even something as simple as a leaf can become the focal point of the breeding site.

Companion species are sometimes permitted into territories. A good

example of this are the 'dither' fish that aquarists introduce to an aquarium when they are trying to breed some of the *Apistogramma* species. The small dither fish, usually tetras, swim around in their normal manner, which makes the cichlids feel secure. They sense that there can be no predators in the vicinity, otherwise the tetras would have long since departed. The tetras themselves, swimming in the mid to upper levels of the aquarium, pose no threat to the cichlids, who are busy on the substrate.

Internal fertilization
In the fishes that practise internal fertilization, the first rays of the anal fin of the male are fused together to form an intromittent organ (also referred to as a gonopodium in the livebearers). Its function is to introduce sperm into the female, thus permitting internal fertilization.

The auchenipterid catfish have such a development of the anal fin on males but, after courtship and copulation, the internally fertilized eggs are expelled by the female and continue their development outside the body, in the same manner as those of the egglayers.

The gonopodium of the livebearers is probably the first feature that novice aquarists learn about when sexing fish, because it is so strikingly different from the anal fin of the females. In most of the South American livebearing cyprinodonts, the freely movable gonopodium may end in either barbs, spines or curved hooks, which seem to be used to help keep the

Left: The tiny male Girardinus metallicus *courts his much larger female, thrusting his gonopodium forward towards her, just before mating. The gestation period lasts about four weeks. Parents eat their fry.*

Above: The young fry can be clearly seen through the body wall of this highly gravid female Xenotoca eisenii. *Given plenty of food in a well-planted tank, the parents will leave the fry alone.*

gonopodium in position while the milt is transferred to the female.

The gonopodium of the male four-eyed fish, *Anableps anableps*, is covered in scales. It is movable, but only to the left or the right, not both. The female's genital opening is covered by a special scale called the foricula, which is attached on one side and free on the other. A problem may arise because in some individuals the opening is on the right, and in others it is on the left. This means that the poor four-eyed female may find herself a real hunky male but he is no use to her because his gonopodium bends the wrong way. So for successful copulation, a righthanded female must find a lefthanded male or vice versa and copulation takes place sideways!

The phallostethids, found from the Malay Peninsular to the Philippines, are another group of livebearers. The male's copulatory organ (the priapium) acts as an intromittent organ. It is a large, fleshy appendage that is found much further forward

119

on the body than would be expected, as it lies just beneath the head and 'chest'. It is supported by a complex internal skeleton. Not only does it house the copulatory organs, but the ducts from the kidneys and intestines also open into it. To aid mating, there are some movable, external bony features and these may help the male hold on to the female. In a similar fashion to the four-eyed fish, the priapium is placed either to the left or right, never symmetrically on the body. With some of the livebearers, the sperm can be stored in the body and used to fertilize more than one brood of youngsters.

Parental care

Parental care takes many forms, from building a nest, which can be anything from a simple scrape in the substrate to an elaborate construction of aquatic vegetation, a raft of bubbles (see page 112), seeking out a cave or hollow, or taking other precautions to ensure that the eggs and subsequent fry grow large enough to be able to fend for themselves.

The type of nest is usually characterized by conditions, for example, the type of substrate, but it is also characteristic of the species constructing it. Nests serve as a place to deposit the eggs. Eggs may remain there for several days, guarded by the parents or just a few moments until one or other parent picks them up into their mouth, or they become attached to part of the body. Sometimes the parent fish excavate more than one nest and the eggs are transferred from pit to pit in the parents' mouths. This also happens with the fry.

Sometimes nests are large affairs. Take for example, the aba (Gymnarchus). This large African mormyrid constructs a substantial floating nest with thick walls. It sticks up out of the water on three sides and on the fourth side is the entrance which may be concealed some 15-20cm (6-8in) below the water surface.

Other fish, such as the African lungfishes Protopterus annectens and P. aethiopicus, dig a deep hole in the substrate or river bank and breed in there. In South America, as the waters recede, large holes can be seen in the river banks and it is in these excavations that some of the larger hypostomid catfish breed.

Aquarists often think that mouthbrooding is the sole preserve of the some of the African cichlids, but it also occurs in the ariid catfishes, the arowana and the Amblyopsidae, a family of blind cave fishes. During the time that the fish are brooding they do not eat.

The South American discus have a unique way of caring for the fry in the weeks after hatching. The embryos leave the eggs and cling on to the flanks of the parents, where they feed on the body mucus. Feeding is shared by both male and

Right: After hatching, young discus feed from the parents' body mucus. Both parents are involved with this and the fry pass freely from one to the other. The young soon take small live foods as well.

Right: A male Sturisoma aureum *guards a brood of eggs attached to the aquarium glass. The fry can be seen developing inside the eggs. Parental duties continue until the eggs hatch.*

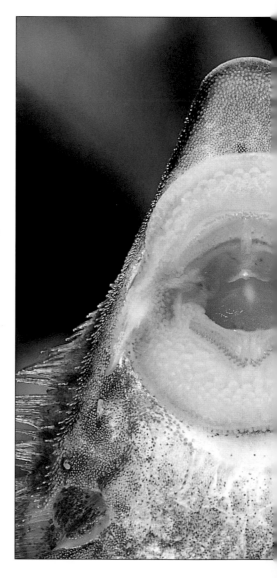

female, with the fry being gently flicked from one parent to the other. Aquarium observations have shown that this can continue for five weeks or more, despite offerings of more conventional small fry foods.

A South American catfish with a strange way of brooding her young is *Platystacus*, a member of the banjo family. As her time for breeding approaches, the female's abdomen becomes very swollen and spongy. After she has laid her eggs and the male has fertilized them, she lays on the eggs and they stick to her belly. Over the next day or so, a stalk with a cup at the end develops to hold each egg (they look like acorns in a cup). Each cup is supplied with blood vessels and these may help nourish the embryo. The eggs remain the cups until they hatch.

In Australia, there is one freshwater species that has taken things to an extreme, the nursery fish, *Kurtus gulliveri*. In this quite large fish it is easy enough to distinguish mature males and females: males have a hook on the forehead. Although precious little is known of their courtship or spawning rituals, males have been caught with small numbers of large eggs dangling from the hooks like a bunch of grapes. They were attached to the hook by cords made from twisted eggs membranes, and clusters of eggs were seen on either side of the male as he swam about.

Growing up
Fish eggs vary greatly, both in size and toughness of the outer membrane, which may be anything from very tough and leathery to very

thin and fragile. Eggs are normally round and contain a yolk. There are two type of eggs: pelagic and demersal. Being lighter than water, pelagic eggs float. The membrane surrounding them is usually thin and non-adhesive. Demersal eggs are heavier than water and, therefore,

sink to the bottom. Their membrane may be smooth and hard or adhesive. For our purposes, the vast majority of freshwater fish eggs are demersal. A notable exception is the butterflyfish, *Pantodon*, which produces eggs that float at the water surface.

Egg size is also a variable. At an average size of about 2mm (0.08in), pelagic eggs are usually much smaller than demersal eggs, and this makes them more difficult to see as they float near the water surface. The aba (*Gymnarchus*) has large eggs about 10mm (0.4in) in diameter. The arriid catfish also have large eggs; records show they can exceed 15mm (0.6in).

Hatching and further development

On hatching, some species are miniature replicas of their parents; they only differ in their lack of maturity. Other species spend only a very short time in the egg and the newly hatched larvae must undergo a term of larval development until

Below: By the time fish are sold in shops they are replicas of adults. If you breed your own fish, however, it is possible to see the development of the unpaired fins from the median fin fold, as shown on this Megalechis thoracatus.

the structure of their bodies resembles that of their parents. As a general rule, the larger the egg, the more developed the post-embryonic fish. This is due to the larger yolk, which supplies the developing embryo with nourishment.

The amount of development at hatching varies a great deal from species to species, but generally speaking this is what happens. When the embryo leaves the egg it is transparent, with a median fin fold that runs along the back around the tail and along the bottom of the fish as far as the vent. To look at (and you will need a good magnifying glass to see this) the median fin fold resembles a single clear fin without any trace of supporting fin spines or rays.

The mouth may not yet be formed. At this stage, the yolk sac is still the food supply and, as it is used up, so the mouth forms and the larvae begins to feed on

REPRODUCTION

Above: Tiny fry of midwater fish, such as these bubblenesting Trichopsis vittatus, *often hang near the surface among fine-leaved plants to avoid predation and benefit from the oxygen-rich waters.*

microorganisms. If you have ever tried breeding fish, you can now see why there is little point in offering food to the fry too soon as they have no mouth to eat it! At such an early stage, the blood is colourless and the gill openings may not be formed.

Soon, the median fin fold begins to break up as the fins develop and the pectoral fins also appear. There is no rule as to which fins develop first; it varies between species.

Development continues until the internal organs, including the skeleton, are fully formed and the young fish looks like a miniature version of its parents. In livebearers (viviparous fish), development is almost completely embryonic. Needless to say, brood numbers are relatively small in these fish, but at birth, the fry are far more able to cope with survival than a newly hatched egglayer.

As a very general rule, fish that produce well-formed young produce fewer eggs or live young than those whose young are poorly developed. Both eggs and fry are food for a large number of creatures, so predation rates are high. It follows that the more highly formed the young, the better their chances of survival, and the parents need produce fewer of them to ensure that at least one or two stand a chance of surviving to maturity to ensure the continuity of the species.

A SCIENTIFIC SUMMARY

Scientists classify all living things into groups. For our purposes the seven main categories are: kingdom (the largest, which includes all below it), phylum, class, order, family, genus and finally the smallest, an individual species.

The fish shown here are from the major groups at the level of **order** encountered by aquarists, but are not all the groups available in the hobby. (Names at the order level always ends in '-iformes', which helps to remind you at what level you are working.) The next level to concern fishkeepers is **family**, which has the ending '-idae'. Then comes the **genus** (the first part of the scientific name), and finally the **specific** name, which identifies the individual fish. Both the generic name and specific name are traditionally shown in *italic* type.

How the section works

The first three orders we look at here – Siluriformes, Characiformes and Cypriniformes – are members of a larger group called the Ostariophysi. They all share the modification of the first four vertebrae into small bones that link the swimbladder to the inner ear. Many species in these orders are also able to release an alarm substance that gives rise to a fright reaction in like species in the vicinity. This large group embraces just over 25% of all known fish and over 70% of freshwater species.

The next two groups of fishes we discuss - cichlids and anabantids – are part of the order Perciformes, which includes both freshwater and marine fish. Of the freshwater Perciformes, it is the cichlids and anabantids that are most often encountered in the hobby.

The final order here is the Cyprinodontiformes, a complex grouping that includes the killifish and livebearers.

Siluriformes – Catfish

This large group of fish (in excess of 30 families and 2,000 species) has become very popular with hobbyists, mainly because of their great diversity. Body form can be anything from torpedo-shaped or triangular in cross-section, to depressed or compressed – all clear indications of lifestyle, be it midwater-swimming, bottom-dwelling, substrate-burying, or open water-swimming, to name but a few. No catfishes have scales, instead they are either covered with a thick skin or have bony plates for protection. Fins are armed with spines that not only serve as a deterrent to predators, but may also be used by some species to lock themselves into crevices. One family has developed the ability to produce electricity. Most are able to produce sound, either by stridulation or with the elastic spring mechanism (see page 92). Most catfish have barbels, but numbers vary greatly. Feeding strategies range from filter feeding to predation. Reproductive strategies include egg-scatterers, egg-depositors, mouthbrooders and those that are internally fertilized but then lay eggs. Some show parental care; others leave the eggs to fend for themselves.

Below: Many species of Corydoras, *such as these* C. paleatus, *are active during the day, especially if kept in groups. They are also one of the easiest catfish to breed.*

Characiformes – Characins

The characins are a large group of diverse species that occur in South America and Africa. South American representatives are more numerous – some 250 genera and in excess of 1,000 species, with more being found all the time.

The African species are contained in about 30 genera, with over 200 species. Many make good aquarium fish but some can be quite delicate, requiring the fishkeeper to pay careful attention to water conditions and feeding. Others, such as the infamous piranha, are more tolerant of tank conditions but need equal care because of their belligerent nature. Most, but by no means all, characins have a rayless adipose fin and teeth. Diets vary greatly; the fish

Left: A typical omnivorous cyprinid, these tiger barbs (Barbus tetrazona) *are shoaling fishes that will eat just about anything, picking at plants, grubbing in the substrate for worms or avidly devouring dried aquarium foods.*

Above: Tetras are probably the most popular of the characins kept in home aquariums. Just looking at an impressive shoal of cardinal tetras (Cheirodon axelrodi) *such as this explains why their popularity never seems to wane.*

may be herbivores, carnivores, insectivores, filter-feeders or scale-eaters, which reflects their diversity. There is a great variety of body shapes and feeding strategies among characins, and they live at all water levels, from hatchetfish at the surface to darters on the substrate.

Cypriniformes

This order includes the following well-known families: Cyprinidae, which includes the barbs, carps, danios, rasboras and minnows;

Cobitidae, the loaches; Balitoridae, the hillstream and river loaches; and Gyrinocheilidae, the algae-eaters. Cyprinids do not have an adipose fin, but they do have a single lateral line, cycloid scales and toothless mouths, using pharyngeal teeth to grind up their food. Depending on species, they may have up to two pairs of barbels. Most hobby fish are typically fish-shaped, shoaling specimens. Size can vary greatly from species to species, from 2-3cm to 2m (0.8-1.2in to 6ft 6in), with larger

species often being caught as food
fish in their native lands. In the
aquarium, the shoaling and breeding
behaviour of this group of fish is
fascinating to observe, especially if
they are kept in suitable numbers in
large tanks. The loaches, hillstream
loaches and algae-eaters are all
bottom-dwelling creatures, often
found in fast-flowing streams. Their
body form is elongate or compressed
– ideally suited to their environment.

Perciformes – Cichlids

Cichlids are found in both fresh and
brackish waters from South America
(they also extend into Texas, USA)
and the West Indies to Africa. They
are also found in Madagascar, Syria
and along the coast of India. They
are extremely popular aquarium fish
and contained in a single family,
Cichlidae. They have a single nostril
on either side, a broken lateral line
and cycloid scales. There are spines

in the anal fin and, amongst those encountered by aquarists, in the dorsal fin, too. Body shape can vary greatly. They have been extensively studied by scientists, who often

Below: The popularity of discus (Symphysodon sp.) has led specialist breeders to develop many new colour, body and finnage forms such as these to fulfil the requirements of the hobby. The true species are now a rare sight.

specialize in a very limited group, such as those from the Rift Valley Lakes of Africa. Research in the field has provided information on their distribution, relationships and diversity of feeding habitats. As these fish enter the hobby, aquarium observations and breeding records have added and continue to add to our knowledge. With over 1,000 species, many of which are suited to aquarium life, cichlids are one of the

best groups of fish to observe in the aquarium. It is fascinating to see how they use their fins, for example, to make tiny manoeuvres involved in breeding displays, parental care and territorial behaviour.

Perciformes – Anabantids

Known within the hobby as the air-breathing fishes, anabantids have an accessory breathing organ that allows them to survive in oxygen-deficient waters. Those encountered by hobbyists are found from Africa into Asia, and belong to various families, of which the most popular include Anabantidae, Belontiidae, Helostomatidae and Osphronemidae. The dorsal and anal fins have spines. Their breeding strategies make them popular aquarium fish. Those that construct bubblenests, such as *Trichogaster* and some species of *Betta*, are regularly bred, while the mouthbrooding species are less well known. Parental care is good, but the fishkeeper must ensure that spent females are not killed by the protective male after spawning is over. The paradisefish *(Macropodus opercularis)* is a long-established fish within the hobby, but the most celebrated is the Siamese fighter *(Betta splendens)*, whose pugnacious attitude has led to it being bred to bring out its fighting tendencies. It has long been used in the Far East in combat, where money changes hands on the outcome of the fight. Even now, there are specialist societies for bettas alone and new colours and forms are still being bred.

Above: *The anabantids can vary in size from the small croaking gouramis through the medium-sized gouramis, such as these* Trichogaster leeri, *to the very large giant gourami. Make sure that you can provide a suitably sized aquarium for the species you wish to keep; only then will you see them at their best.*

Cyprinodontiformes – Killifish and Livebearers

This category is easily split for our purposes into the egglaying toothcarps (the killifish) and livebearing toothcarps (the livebearers). The problem arises when you start to look at the breeding strategies of some livebearers and discover that some practise internal fertilization but then produce eggs! In the hobby, we will encounter killifish from the families Aplocheilidae, Profundulidae and Fundulidae. Killifish are found in the Americas, Africa and parts of Asia. They are egglayers; some hang their eggs on plants, while others bury them in the substrate (see page 109). Males of most species are easy to distinguish from females because they are far more colourful. Because females of similar species are easily confused, killifishes are usually kept in separate species aquariums to avoid interbreeding taking place.

The livebearers most often seen are from the families Goodeidae, Poeciliidae, Cyprinodontidae and Anablepidae. It is from this group of fish that some of the most popular aquarium fish arise. Guppies, mollies, swordtails and platies have long been the mainstay of the hobby and their ease of breeding has led to many manmade varieties being produced. In recent years, however, the true species have gained popularity. Aquarium breeding is not always straightforward, but sexing is easy; in the male the anal fin is modified to a greater or lesser extent into an intromittent organ. In addition, there may be a great difference in size between the sexes. Like killifishes, some livebearers will readily cross-breed and serious hobbyists maintain their stocks in species tanks.

Left: *Male killifish are among the most attractive fish in the hobby, but they need care and patience. Water conditions and feeding can be demanding, but the joy of breeding them make it all worthwhile.*

Above: *Platies have been hybridized to produce many colour forms and finnage shapes. Some are not as robust as the wild species and require careful attention paid to water quality.*

INDEX

CREDITS

The publishers would like to thank the following photographers for providing images, credited here by page number and position: B(Bottom), T(Top), C(Centre), BL(Bottom left), etc.

M P & C Piednoir/Aqua Press: Title page, 8, 12, 14(J M Londiveau), 15(T,C), 16, 17, 20, 21(T), 24, 27(C,BR), 28, 29(T,B), 34, 41, 42, 43, 47, 52, 53, 54-55, 60, 63, 66, 67, 71, 72, 73(T), 76, 80, 82-83(T), 84, 85, 86, 87(TR), 90, 92, 94(T), 100(T), 102, 104, 105, 107, 109, 110, 111(B), 113, 114, 115, 116, 116-117(B), 118, 119, 121, 122-123, 125, 127, 128(BL), 128-129(T), 130-131, 132-133, 134
Dave Bevan: 18, 44-45(B), 135
Arend van den Nieuwenhuizen: 10, 13, 19, 25, 38-39, 45(T), 65, 82(B), 108, 111(T), 112
Photomax (Max Gibbs): 22(C), 91, 98-99(T), 103
Geoffrey Rogers © Interpet Publishing: Half title page, 21(CR), 32, 33, 48, 58, 61, 70, 89, 94(B)
Mike Sandford: 22(T), 31(T,C), 57, 73(CR), 87(CL), 96, 97, 100-101(B), 124
W A Tomey: 26-27(T), 35, 64
The artwork illustrations have been prepared by Phil Holmes and Stuart Watkinson and are © Interpet Publishing.

ACKNOWLEDGMENTS

The author would like to thank Gordon Howes and Keith Banister for their infectious enthusiasm and patience.
The publishers acknowledge that the illustrations featured in this book have been based on the following sources: *Vertebrate Life* by F. Harvey Pough, Christine M. Janis and John B. Heiser, published by Prentice-Hall Inc., New Jersey, 1999. *The Biology of Fishes* by Q. Bone, N.B. Marshall and J.H.S. Blaxter, published by Stanley Thornes (Publishers) Ltd., Cheltenham, 1999. *The Vertebrate Eye* by G.L. Walls, published by Hafner, New York, 1963